NOW YOU CAN BE
A MASTER OF MAGIC

It doesn't matter if you're a young person seeking to startle family, friends and the world, or an adult wanting to delight the kids.

It doesn't matter if you've never tried magic before, or are an old hand at sleight-of-hand.

It doesn't matter if you don't have any equipment beyond common everyday objects and don't have much time or any money to spend.

All that matters is here in the greatest guide to instant magic mastery ever offered. Clearly written and wonderfully illustrated, these 101 SEPARATE, SURE-FIRE SUPER TRICKS will enthrall and mystify every audience, whether in the living room, at the dinner table, or on the stage.

101
BEST MAGIC
TRICKS

FIND THE ANSWERS!

☐ **101 BEST MAGIC TRICKS by Guy Frederick.** Top magician Guy Frederick lets you into the inner circle of those who know what others never can even guess about how magic really works. Includes handkerchief tricks, card tricks, mind reading tricks, and much much more! (158598—$3.50)

☐ **THE COMPLETE BOOK OF MAGIC AND WITCHCRAFT by Kathryn Paulsen.** The unique guide to everything you need to know to become a witch— with all the ancient and modern recipes, spells, and incantations essential for magic, witchcraft and sorcery. (168321—$4.95)

☐ **WEDDINGS: A COMPLETE GUIDE TO ALL RELIGIOUS AND INTERFAITH MARRIAGE SERVICES by Abraham J. Klausner.** The Essential Handbook for every couple planning a wedding or renewal vows. "A significant work!"—S. Burtner Ulrich, Rector, St. John's Episcopal Church, Yonkers, N.Y. (153898—$3.95)

☐ **HOW TO BUY A CAR FOR ROCK-BOTTOM PRICE by Dr. Leslie R. Sachs.** Get the lowdown from the man who went undercover as a car salesman to learn the tricks of the trade. What you don't know about buying a car could cost you thousands. (149610—$3.95)

☐ **HOW TO KNOW THE BIRDS by Roger Tory Peterson.** Here is an authoritative, on-the-spot guide to help you recognize instantly most American birds on sight. Includes a 24-page color supplement. (129393—$4.50)

☐ **THE AMATEUR MAGICIAN'S HANDBOOK by Henry Hay.** Fourth revised edition. A professional magician teaches you hundreds of the tricks of his trade in this unsurpassed, illustrated guide. (155025—$4.95)

Prices slightly higher in Canada

Buy them at your local bookstore or use this convenient coupon for ordering.

NEW AMERICAN LIBRARY
P.O. Box 999, Bergenfield, New Jersey 07621

Please send me the books I have checked above. I am enclosing $_____
(please add $1.00 to this order to cover postage and handling). Send check or money order—no cash or C.O.D.'s. Prices and numbers are subject to change without notice.

Name_____

Address_____

City _____ State _____ Zip Code _____
Allow 4-6 weeks for delivery.
This offer, prices and numbers are subject to change without notice.

101
BEST MAGIC
TRICKS

By Guy Frederick

Illustrated by
Doug Anderson

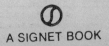

A SIGNET BOOK

SIGNET
Published by the Penguin Group
Penguin Books USA Inc., 375 Hudson Street,
New York, New York 10014, U.S.A.
Penguin Books Ltd, 27 Wrights Lane,
London W8 5TZ, England
Penguin Books Australia Ltd, Ringwood,
Victoria, Australia
Penguin Books Canada Ltd, 2801 John Street,
Markham, Ontario, Canada L3R 1B4
Penguin Books (N.Z.) Ltd, 182-190 Wairau Road,
Auckland 10, New Zealand

Penguin Books Ltd, Registered Offices:
Harmondsworth, Middlesex, England

Published by Signet, an imprint of New American Library,
a division of Penguin Books USA Inc.

This is an authorized reprint of a hardcover edition published
by Sterling Publishing Co., Inc.

First Signet Printing, December, 1979
15   14   13   12   11   10   9   8   7

 REGISTERED TRADEMARK—MARCA REGISTRADA

Printed in the United States of America

Contents

Introduction

Magic is fun for everyone. If you know several good magic tricks, everyone will want to see them. After people know you can do magic, you will always be asked to bring along your "bag of tricks."

Here you will find 101 of the best tricks and they are all easy to do! There are tricks with everyday articles you have around the house, tricks that you can do without preparation, and a section on "do-it-yourself" magic.

Magic is not hard to do once you are "in the know." Sometimes the simpler the explanation of the trick, the more difficult it will be for people to figure out.

Concentrate on learning just a few tricks to begin with. Once you get the knack, you'll want to include all 101 in your repertoire. You can have lots of fun fooling your family and friends. Everybody likes to be fooled—it's fun to be fooled. But it's more fun to fool!

1.
Fundamental Tricks

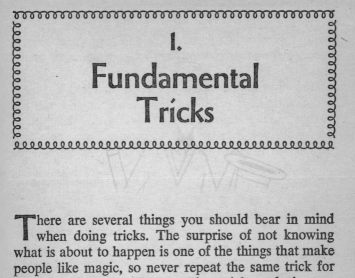

There are several things you should bear in mind when doing tricks. The surprise of not knowing what is about to happen is one of the things that make people like magic, so never repeat the same trick for the same audience. Have another trick ready in case you are asked to show the first trick again.

Never tell what you are going to do before you start a trick, because if you do, it will be easier for your audience to see how you do a trick, and that spoils the fun. Keep them fooled!

Don't expose the workings of a trick after you have done it, or a fellow-magician either. It's more fun to keep your friends guessing, because magic isn't magic to people who know what methods you use.

You may present your magic in a natural, comic, or mysterious way. In the natural way of presentation you should strive to be yourself and not imitate anyone else. Be casual and easy-going. This is usually the best way to perform your magic before a group of people you know well.

The comic style is used if you are before a larger group and have a natural flair for comedy. You should joke with your audience, but never poke fun at them—laugh with them—not at them. Remember,

1

your audience is every bit as ready to be entertained as to be fooled. Comedy is a good form of entertainment. Remember though, not to be a show-off or act smart-alecky.

The mysterious style is usually best suited to a large stage and, as a rule, to an older person. If you are naturally very serious, and are really not the type to be funny, you may be able to present your show in a mysterious manner. Don't try to be too mysterious or you may end up being funny.

Don't mix the styles of presentation; either be natural, funny or mysterious.

Patter is the name magicians give to the running line of talk they use while they are performing a trick. It's a good idea for you to learn to keep up a continuous flow of chatter or patter as you perform because this will make your magic more interesting and entertaining.

You should not memorize what you are going to say. Just get an idea of what you want to say as you perform. Then fill in with what comes to your mind as you do your shows. This will only come with practice. You may tell certain things that you may do, or call attention to the various articles you use. This is, of course, just the beginning. You must say other things in between so that your show will not have "dead spots" in it. All of your patter must be in the same style as your presentation, such as: natural, comedy, or mysterious. Some tricks have a story attached to them naturally such as the Four Robbers Trick (page 8), and the Afghan Bands (page 115). Try most of all to be original in your stories and don't copy other magicians you may see. It is not only unfair to take someone else's patter, but it probably won't fit your style of magic.

If you are going to do a complete show and not just a few tricks, it is important to arrange them in a good program. The opening trick is the most important because it introduces you to your audience and makes them either expect to see a good magician or one not so good. You should choose a trick that is quick and attention-getting. Do not use a trick which requires the use of spectators from the audience, but one that you can do quickly and that will baffle the audience.

The last trick should be fast and colorful as well as mysterious as it is the last time the audience sees you, and you want them to remember you as a pleasant person with lots of skill and talent.

Your dress is also important. The best thing for a boy to wear is a suit with a tie. Also, be neat and clean in your appearance, as this will make the audience like you better when they first see you. Boys will find coat pockets handy in many of the tricks. Girls can wear slacks and a coat, or a skirt or a smock with pockets.

Magicians use a language all their own. You will find some of these terms useful and interesting, and they form the basis of a great many tricks. If you want to fool your audience you will have to practice certain tricks until you can do them without hesitating. You will find references to the following "Fundamental Tricks" throughout the rest of this book.

Palming is holding something in your hand without the audience's knowing it is there. The easiest "palm" is called the finger-palm because the object is held in the natural curl of your two middle fingers. With a small object, such as a coin or a ball, held this way, you can move your hand freely and naturally. Your

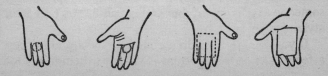

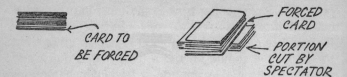

CARD TO BE FORCED

FORCED CARD

PORTION CUT BY SPECTATOR

arm can be held in front of your body, or dropped to your side without the object's falling out.

Forcing is causing a spectator to pick a certain card when he thinks he has a free choice. To "force" a card, place the card you wish to force on the bottom of the deck—that is, under the last card of the deck. Hold the deck on the palm of your hand, and ask the spectator to cut the deck at any point he wishes. Have him place the part he cut, and now holds, on the palm of his hand.

Place the portion you hold, crosswise on top of the portion in his hand. Ask him to pick up the top part of the deck (the one you have placed crosswise) and look at the bottom, or face-up card. To him it appears as if this was the card he cut to, but it is really the card that was on the bottom of the deck at the beginning—in other words, the "force" card.

This may sound very simple. It is, and because it is so simple, it really fools them. Try it and see!

Another Force is called the "bridge" force. Place the card to be forced on the bottom of the deck. Cut the deck at about the center, and bend the top packet along the ends in a concave "bridge." Now complete the cut and place the unbent portion on top of the bent portion.

Ask the spectator to cut the cards near the center, and glance at the card on the bottom of the packet to which he has cut. He will cut to the force card.

Before doing this, it is a good idea to notice whether he cuts the cards at the sides or the ends. This

FORCE CARD

will work very well if he cuts at the sides, but if he cuts at the ends, you must bend the cards at the *sides* when you cut. Most people cut at the sides.

The Pass is a very difficult but skillful trick which is used to bring a selected card to the top of the deck. This lets the spectator take any card from the deck, replace it, and lets you bring it to the top. This variation of the pass is very easy.

Fan the cards out and have someone select a card. Square up the deck and cut it at about the center. Ask the spectator to return his card, by placing it on top of the bottom pack, in your left hand. Hold the pack in the palm of your hand with the fingers curled around one side and the thumb on the other.

Replace the packet from your right hand on top of the one in your left, but as you do so, slip the tip of

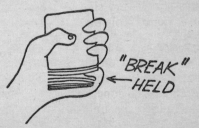

"BREAK" ←HELD

your left little finger in between the two packets. Riffle the outer ends of the cards a few times but keep looking right into the eyes of the spectator. *Do not look at your hands*.

Grasp the ends of the cards with your right fingers

at the front, thumb at the back, and cut the cards at the break held by your little finger.

Now riffle shuffle the cards, being sure the top card on the packet held in your left hand falls on top. This will be the selected card. You can shuffle some more, but you can always locate the card very easily, as you will keep it on the top of the deck.

The One-Way Principle means using a deck which has a picture or figure on the back which is non-reversible. The back design has a definite top and bottom (rather than a pattern which looks the same in either direction) and you can tell if one of the cards is upside down.

To use this principle, arrange the cards so that the back designs face all one way. Fan the cards and have someone in the audience remove one. If you fan the cards in your left hand from left to right (top to bottom), and someone selects one, continue to close the fan in the same direction. If you use the left thumb and fingers as a pivot, you will find that when you square up the cards, you will have turned them completely around.

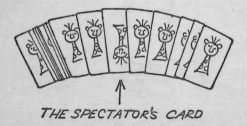

THE SPECTATOR'S CARD

Have the card returned to the deck, and let the spectator shuffle them, or shuffle them yourself. Now fan the cards face-out toward the spectator, and have him make sure his card is in the deck. While he is looking for his card it is easy for you to find it, too, as it will be the only one with an upside down pattern!

The Key-Card Principle is nothing more than using one card to locate another. To use this principle, note the bottom card of the pack. Have a spectator select a card.

While he is looking at it, cut the cards, and ask him to replace his card on top of the pile you have cut from the deck. Now complete the cut. This puts the bottom card that you remembered, the key-card, directly over his selected card.

Now turn the deck face-up in your hands and look for your key-card. You will find the selected card to the right of your key-card.

In the following chapter, you will find tricks in which these principles are used, and also many others which you will find just as easy to do.

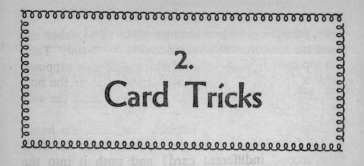

2.
Card Tricks

Tricks with playing cards are the most popular magic tricks today. Many can be done without long hours of practice. The tricks in this book are good tricks, and easy to do. Later in the book are more tricks that depend not upon sleight of hand, but on special preparation. These will be found in the chapter on advanced magic.

The Four Robbers

Hold up four Jacks, which represent four robbers. Tell your audience that the Jacks decide to rob a house, which is represented by the deck. You will place the robbers in different parts of the house, but at the end of the trick they will all appear back together at the top of the house.

Before you start, all you need to do is place any three cards behind the Jacks before you fan them out to show them. Fan out only the Jacks, and keep the three extra cards hidden behind the Jacks.

Now start your patter. Say, "Here are four robbers named Jack, who decided to rob a house. We'll let the deck of cards represent the house." Place the Jacks, with the extra cards on top of them, on top of the deck, facedown. Then continue. "The first robber entered the house through a window in the cellar." Take the top card from the deck (which everyone supposes to be a Jack) and push it into the deck near the bottom. Don't let anyone see its face. Push it all the way in, so that it is lost.

Now say, "The second robber went into the house by the front door." Take the top card from the deck (the second indifferent card) and push it into the deck near the center. "The third robber entered the house by the back door." Take the top card again and place it in the deck near the center. "The fourth robber stayed right here on the roof to act as the lookout." Pick up the top card and show it to the audience. Of course, this really is the first of the four Jacks. Now replace it on the top of the deck.

Continue your story. "The police came and the lookout warned the other robbers, and, what do you know? Here are all four robbers back on the roof!" As you say this, deal the four Jacks, one at a time, from the top of the deck onto the table, face-up, so that everybody can see them.

The Four Aces

In this trick, you hand the spectator a deck of cards, and have him cut it into four equal piles. Then you ask him to transfer numerous cards back and forth from pile to pile and after the cards are seemingly lost and hopelessly mixed-up, the spectator finds an Ace on top of each pile.

The preparation for this trick is very easy. Before you start the trick place the four Aces on top of the deck. Now hand the deck to a spectator and make clear to him that he is going to do this trick; you won't even touch the cards.

Have him cut the deck into four equal piles. Most people cut from left to right, and in all likelihood the pile on his right will be the one with Aces on top. The only thing you must watch is to see where he puts the top pile. Now you try to confuse the spectator by having him move cards around from one pile to another in a seemingly aimless manner. However, you really keep track of the Aces as they are moved. What you want to do is to end with an Ace on top of each pile.

I won't give you any set way of moving the cards, because you probably won't do the trick exactly the same way any time you do it. It would be very hard to follow a pattern anyway, so just to give you an idea, let's call the pile to the spectator's left No. 1 and so

on. Pile No. 4 will be the one with the Aces. Start by having the spectator take a card from No. 2 and put it on No. 3. Then take one card from No. 2 and place it on No. 1.

As you perform the trick, don't refer to the piles by number. Just point to them and say, "Take the card from the top of this pile and place it on that pile." You can have him move the cards back and forth as many times as you wish but be sure to keep your eye on the Aces. This may sound confusing, but try it and you will see how easy it is to do, and how baffling! But be sure to get an Ace on each pile before you finish the trick.

Another Ace Trick

This is an interesting trick which uses four Aces again. Aces are the highest value cards in most card games and always appeal to an audience.

In this trick you deal the four Aces onto the table, and place three indifferent cards on top of each Ace. Have a spectator select one of the piles, and meanwhile the Aces vanish from the other piles and appear in the selected pile.

To start the trick, place the four Aces on top of the deck, then on top of these place any three cards, as you did in "The Four Robbers" trick. Hold up the four Aces (really seven cards) and show them to your audience. Place the cards on top of the deck.

Deal the top four cards onto the table making four piles. Deal the first card to your left, the second to the right of this, and the third card on your right, leaving room between the second and fourth piles for the fourth card, the first Ace. Now take three cards from the top of the deck (the three Aces) and place them casually on top of the third pile, really on top of the

first Ace. Now place three more cards on top of each
of the other piles.

You now have four piles of four cards each. To the
audience it looks as though you have four piles with
an Ace in each.

Now ask a spectator to select a number between
one and four. He can't say one or four, because you
asked for a number *between* one and four. This leaves
him numbers two or three. If he says two, count the
piles from right to left, "one, two." If he says three,
count from left to right, "one, two, three," and you
will end up on the pile containing the four Aces. Push
this pile slightly forward. Now turn over the cards in
pile number one. Show the spectators that the Ace has
vanished! Repeat this with the other two piles and
now you are left with the pile selected by the
spectator.

Emphasize that this is the pile he has selected. Turn
the cards over quickly, one at a time, and show that
the Aces have traveled to the selected pile.

A Simple Reverse

*Have someone select a card, and replace it in the
deck. Upon spreading the cards out on the table, one
card will be face-down; it will be the card that was
selected.*

Before you start the trick, turn the bottom card

over so that it faces the rest of the cards in the pack. Fan the deck slightly, so as not to expose the turned-over card.

Have someone select a card, and while the spectator is looking at it, secretly turn over the deck so that the bottom or reversed card is at the top of the deck. It will look as if this was the top of the deck. Have the spectator replace the card in the pack, but hold the pack firmly so that he cannot see the other cards in the deck.

Turn around and go to a table, and as you do so, turn the bottom card over so that it will be facing the same way as the rest of the cards. Spread the cards face-up on the table. One card will be reversed. Ask the spectator to name his card. He does so, and you will then turn over the face-down card, which proves to be the card he selected.

Something on Your Mind

This is a "quickie" and is a gag as well as a trick.

Have someone select a card and get it to the top of the deck as explained in *The Pass*, page 5.

Have the spectator concentrate on his card. Hold the deck in your right hand and place the deck firmly against your forehead, card-faces toward the spectator. This will put the selected card against your head. Press the deck against your forehead hard, and push upward at the same time. Now tell the spectator that the card is on his mind, and it is also on yours. Remove the deck in an upward sweep, and his card will really be "on your mind," stuck to your forehead.

Usually, the card will stick by itself. It will stick better if you moisten your forefinger and get just a bit of moisture on the top card.

Spell It!

Here is a clever way of revealing a selected card. It is revealed by spelling the name of the card.

Have someone select a card, and get it on top of the deck as explained in *The Pass*, page 5. Ask the spectator to name the card. Deal one card face down on top of the table for each letter spelled. The first card placed face down will be the selected card, but you must continue to deal cards until you have named each letter. If the card was the two of clubs, deal the top card—face down—onto the table and say "t", the next card, "w," then "o" and "o-f—c-l-u-b-s."

Now you turn up the last card, which would be the "s" card, and show it to the spectator. It is not his card. Pretend to be embarrassed and say that you forgot to tap the deck!

Pick up the cards from the table, and replace them on top of the deck. The selected card was on the bottom of the pile on the table, and will be buried in the deck when the cards are replaced.

Hand the deck to the spectator, tap it with your forefinger, and ask *him* to spell out the name of his card, the same way you did, dealing one card for each letter. When he finishes, he will end with his card.

The Red and the Black

In this trick you are able to predict the cards in certain piles dealt by the spectator, even though you never touch the cards. You will first write a prediction on a slip of paper and either place it in full view of the audience, or have another spectator hold it.

Hand a spectator the deck of cards, and have him shuffle them thoroughly. Now have him deal the cards in pairs face-up onto the table. If he comes to two black cards, he is to place them in one pile, if he comes to two red cards, he is to place them in another pile. If he turns up a red one and a black one together, he is to discard them and lay them face-down.

When he has finished dealing the cards, he is to count the red cards, and the black cards. When he reads your prediction he will find that you have written, "You will have two more red cards than black ones," and he does.

How does this happen? Before you hand him the deck remove two black cards from the deck and secretly place them in your pocket. Then write the prediction as above. If you wish, you may remove two red cards, and then your prediction should read, "You will have two more black cards than red ones."

Card From the Pocket

A spectator deals three cards face-up from the deck and selects one, mentally. You place the three cards in your pocket and then withdraw two. The spectator will name his card, which you will draw from your pocket. Then show that your pocket is empty.

Before you start the trick, place any two cards in your right hand trouser pocket. Push the cards to the top inner corner of the pocket, and you will be able to

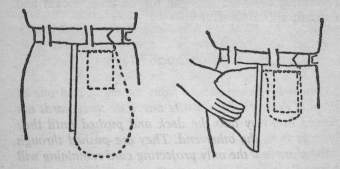

pull out your pocket and show that it is empty. The cards should face toward your body.

Hand the spectator a deck of cards and ask him to shuffle them. Have him deal any three cards face-up onto the table, and select one just by thinking of it. Pick up the cards, and remember the location of each. The easiest way to do this is to pick up the one of highest value first, then the next lower one, and finally place the lowest value card on top, face-down.

After showing that your pocket is empty place the cards in it and appear to concentrate on the spectator's thoughts. Remove the two cards that you placed in your pocket before the start of the trick, and put them into the center of the deck without showing them.

Now ask the spectator to name his card aloud for the first time. Since you know the location of the cards in your pocket, it will be easy to pull out the one he names. The highest card will be closest to your body, while the lowest will be toward the spectator. Pull the card out quickly after it is named, without fumbling, because the audience believes that you have only one card in your pocket. Lay the card down on the table in front of the spectator, face-down. Ask him to turn it over. Reach back into your pocket and push the two remaining cards up into the top of your pocket and casually show it is empty.

The Push-Through Mystery

Three cards are picked from the deck, and one of them is declared the favorite one. The three cards are placed half-way into the deck and pushed until they emerge from the other end. They are pushed through once more and the only projecting card remaining will be the favorite one selected.

This trick works itself. You need to know the card selected by the spectator. Have him pick three cards from the deck. Now lay them face-up on the table in front of him. Ask him to name his favorite card. Fan the deck face-up in front of you and place the first card half-way down into the deck. Now skip two or three cards and place the selected card half-way into

the deck. Skip two or three more cards and place the last card half-way into the deck.

Square up the cards and you will have the three cards projecting from the top of the pack. Hold the deck firmly and tap the protruding cards into the deck. Some cards will project from the bottom. Quickly and firmly push these cards back up. The selected card will be the only one protruding from the deck. Remove it and show it to the spectator.

Another way to finish this is to tap the cards into the deck, then wrap the deck in a handkerchief, so that the top half protrudes. Now under cover of the handkerchief, push upward on the cards that project from the bottom and the selected card will rise from the center of the deck.

The Rising Card

A card is selected and returned to the deck. You hold the deck in your left hand and place your right forefinger above the deck. The card will then rise from the deck.

Have someone select a card and return it to the deck. Bring it to the top as explained in *The Pass*, page 5. Hold the deck by the long edges, in your left hand, with the faces of the cards against your fingers. (This position will hide the lower portion of the deck.)

Place your right hand behind the deck and extend your right forefinger over the top of the deck. Keep the two middle fingers of your right hand bent double, but extend your little finger, under cover of the deck, and push it against the back of the top card. Raise your right hand slowly and mysteriously and the top-selected card will rise from the deck.

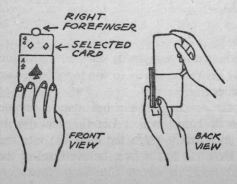

RIGHT FOREFINGER

SELECTED CARD

FRONT VIEW

BACK VIEW

Keep the forefinger just barely touching the top of the card as a guide. It will appear as if you had magnetized your finger and it has attracted the card and caused it to rise from the deck.

The Magician "Nose"

This trick is similar to the last one, in that you cause a card to rise. Use them at different times, not together.

Follow the method used in the last trick and with the selected card on the top of the deck, place the deck, face of cards toward the audience, up against your nose. By placing the tip of your nose near the bottom of the deck and slowly lowering the deck and raising your head slightly, the card will rise from the pack, as you use your nose as a pivot.

You can make up a funny patter—about how "nosy" you are, for instance, or how "the nose knows." This one always gets a laugh.

Cards From the Hat

Here is a clever finish to a card trick. One or several cards are selected, returned to the deck, and the deck is then placed in a fedora hat. You tap the bottom of the hat and the selected card flies into the air, while the deck remains inside.

Have one or several cards selected and returned to the deck. Bring the cards to the top of the deck. See *The Pass*, page 5.

Keep the opening of the hat toward yourself and place the deck in the hat. Let the deck go into one section, and slide the selected card (s) into the other section. Hold the hat above the eye-level of the audience and make a sharp flip with your forefinger

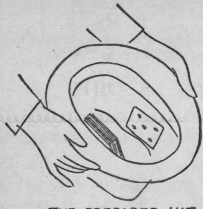

THE PREPARED HAT

against the crown of the hat on the side where the selected card has been placed. The force of the flip causes the card to fly out of the hat in a most mysterious way. Tip the hat over and let the rest of the deck fall onto the table. This trick is more effective if you use a borrowed hat.

HOW THE
TRICK LOOKS

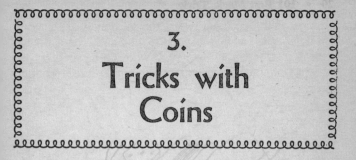

3.
Tricks with Coins

Coin tricks are always interesting because everyone likes money. For these tricks you should use half-dollar-size coins, unless you are specifically told to use another size. If you wish, you can buy "palming coins" in a magic store. Most magicians use these for tricks done on the stage, when the audience can't see them closely. You might also use a "lucky piece" which lots of people carry. You could tell your audience that the coin, besides being lucky, has other magic properties.

The French Drop

This is not really a trick in itself, but is the basis for many coin tricks. You can also use this principle for small objects other than coins, such as balls or keys. The French Drop is really an easy way to make a coin vanish. You seem to pass a coin from one hand to your other one, while really keeping it in the first hand.

Hold the coin by its edges in your left hand between the tips of your fingers and thumb. The flat side of the coin should be parallel to your palm. Point the fingers of your left hand slightly upward so that the flat side of the coin is toward the audience. Hold your left hand still and move your right hand, palm down, toward your left hand as if you were going to take the coin out of your left hand. Your right thumb should

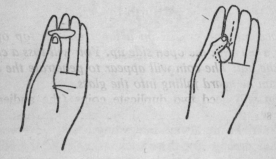

go under the coin and your fingers above it, which hides the coin momentarily. When the coin is hidden, release it and allow it to fall back into your left hand where it should rest on the second joints of your left fingers. Hold it for a moment with your left thumb to keep it from falling.

Now bring your right thumb up along your left finger-tips. Close your right hand is if it held the coin. Move your right hand up and away from your left. As you do this, drop your left hand (with the coin) casually to your side. Be sure to keep your eyes on your right hand. Never look at your left hand. This is what magicians call "misdirection." Now get the coin into the finger-palm position. See *Palming*, page 3.

The movement of seeming to take the coin from your left hand should be one continuous motion. Don't hesitate, except just long enough to seem to take the coin into the right hand. This will require some practice, but it is not hard to do, and will be worth the trouble to learn.

Now, with your right hand held at eye-level, rub your thumb and fingers together. It will look as if the coin dissolved. In some other tricks, you will learn how to get rid of the coin in your left hand, so that you may show both hands are empty.

Coin Through the Hat

Place an empty glass on a table and on top of it place a hat with the open side up. You will toss a coin into the hat. The coin will appear to penetrate the hat and can be heard falling into the glass.

You will need two duplicate coins (the audience must see only one), a glass tumbler, and a hat. (A derby is best, but any man's hat can be used. Borrow one from someone in the audience.) Palm a coin in the finger-palm position in the right hand. See *Palming*, page 3. Show the glass and pick up the hat in your left hand and place it crown down in the right hand right on top of the coin. Now allow the coin to slip down to the tips of your right fingers under cover of the hat. Using both hands, place the hat on top of the glass, so that the coin is held on the edge of the glass by the weight of the hat.

Pick up the other coin, the duplicate coin, in the left hand, perform the *French Drop* (see page 21) and retain the coin in the left hand. Make a throwing motion toward the hat with the right hand, gently touching the rim of the hat, and the coin will fall into the glass. Pick up the hat in the right hand and at the same time slip the coin from your left hand into your pocket. Now place the hat aside and pick up the glass. Let the coin in the glass fall into the hands of a spectator. It will look as though you caused the coin to travel through the hat.

Coin Through the Napkin

You cause a borrowed coin to penetrate a borrowed napkin or handkerchief.

Borrow a coin and have the owner mark it if he wishes.

Hold the coin vertically by its flat side between thumb and forefinger of your left hand. Place the napkin over it so that the coin is under its center. Under cover of the napkin get a small fold of the napkin between your thumb and the coin. Now with your right hand lift the part of the napkin closest to the audience and drape it back on top of the other half, over your left arm, and show that the coin is still there. With a snap of the left wrist, cause both halves of the napkin to fall forward while still holding the coin and the napkin, in the center, in the left hand.

Twist the napkin to give the illusion that the coin is wrapped securely in the center of the napkin. Exert a little pressure on the edge of the coin and it will rise through the napkin. It looks as if it is slowly penetrat-

ing the napkin. Hand the coin back to the spectator
and show that the napkin is unharmed.

Multiplying Money

*You count a number of coins into the hand of a
spectator and apparently "catch" three coins from the
air, and place them in the spectator's hand. When he
opens his hand, he has three more coins than when he
started.*

You will need thirteen coins and a magazine the
size of the *Reader's Digest*.

Before you start the trick, secretly place three coins
under the cover of the magazine, so that they are
hidden.

Hand the ten coins to a spectator and ask him to
count them out loud, one at a time, and place them on
the magazine. Hold the magazine so that the coins will
not fall off. Stress the fact that you are using the magazine so that you do not touch the coins. After he has
counted the coins onto the magazine, have him cup
his hands together to catch the coins. Slightly curl the
magazine to make a little trough, and pour the coins
into his hands. (Of course the three duplicate coins
that you hid under the magazine cover will fall into
his hands, too.) Tell him to close his hands tightly so
that nothing can get in or out.

Reach up into the air and pretend to grab an invisible coin. Hold it up as if you really see it, and ask the
spectator if he can see the coin. Make a throwing motion toward his hand as if you were throwing the coin
into his hand. Ask him if he felt the coin go into his
hands. Ask him, too, if the coins are getting heavier.
Repeat the throwing business two more times. Now
ask him how many coins he had to start with. He will
say ten. Have him open his hands and count the coins
onto the magazine again. He will now have thirteen.

If you wish, you may use borrowed coins. Have a spectator count the coins from his pocket onto the magazine. If he has over seven coins, go on with the trick. If he has less than seven add three from your pocket. The reason for this is that if he has just a few coins to start with, he will be able to tell that you have added coins from the magazine. If you decide to use borrowed coins, have a penny, a nickel, and a dime concealed in the magazine at the beginning of the trick.

The Warm Coin

You borrow several coins. One is scratched to mark it from the rest. The coins are placed in a hat and mixed. Without looking, you are able to reach in and produce the marked coin.

First, stick a small pellet of beeswax on the tip of your thumbnail. Collect the coins and have someone select one, and make a mark or scratch on it for identification. As you take the coin back, press the wax to the edge of the coin and drop it into the hat. Drop the other coins in and have someone mix them up by shaking the hat. Then have him hold the hat up above your eye-level so you cannot see into it. Reach in and feel for the wax. Take out the coin and scrape the wax off with your thumbnail before handing it to the spectators for identification.

Novel Coin Vanish

A coin, placed in a fold of your trousers, vanishes mysteriously.

Take a coin, either real or fake, and attach a foot-long piece of strong thin elastic to it by boring a small hole in the coin. Loop the other end of the elastic through a safety pin. Pin this to the inside of your right coat sleeve so that when the coin hangs down, it will be 2 or 3 inches above the cuff. Place a coin of the same size in your right trouser pocket.

Get the coin from your sleeve and hold it with your right thumb and forefinger, so that the elastic is hidden. Show the coin and place it on your right trouser leg right over the coin in your pocket.

Now with your left hand grasp the cloth of your trousers including the coin in your pocket. Fold the cloth over the coin on the elastic so that it is hidden. Release the pressure on your right hand and the coin will fly up your sleeve.

Have the spectator feel the coin through the cloth of your trousers or tap it with a pencil or key. It will appear as if the coin were still there, but actually it is the coin hidden in your pocket which he feels. Brush your right hand over the spot where the coin is and release the cloth with your left hand. Immediately show both hands empty. With a little practice in front of your mirror, this will be smooth and mysterious.

The Dissolving Coin

A spectator drops a coin in a glass of water while it is covered with a handkerchief. When the handkerchief is removed, the coin has vanished.

Hold a glass about half full of water on your left palm. Have someone place a coin in the center of a handkerchief and then pick up the coin through the handkerchief. Tell him to drape the handkerchief over the glass and drop the coin into the water on your signal. As he does this, tip the glass toward you so that the coin strikes the edge of the glass and falls into your fingers. The noise sounds as if the coin fell into the glass.

Now have the spectator let go of the handkerchief and as you remove it from the glass, allow the coin to slide directly under the center of the glass. Remove the handkerchief and allow him to look directly into the glass and see that the coin is still there.

Cover the glass with the handkerchief again and pick up the glass with your right hand, through the handkerchief. Turn your left hand over so that the coin does not show and finger-palm it (see *Palming*, page 3). Then, still holding the coin in your left hand, lift the handkerchief from the glass and show that the coin has disappeared.

A Quickie Coin Vanish

You vanish a coin by rubbing it into the back of your left hand.

Show the coin to the audience, then place it on the back of your left hand, and rub it from side to side with your right hand. Pretend to drop the coin accidentally on the floor, apologize, and bend over to pick it up. As you start to bring the coin up drop it into your right trouser cuff. Keep bringing your hand up as if it held the coin. Pretend to place the coin on the back of your left hand again and continue rubbing. Now show that the coin has vanished. When picking up the coin, do not pause as you drop it in the cuff. It must look like one smooth operation.

Elbow Coin Vanish

A coin is rubbed into your elbow where it vanishes.

This is best done while you are seated at a table. Drop a coin onto the table and say that it is a magic coin. Bend your left arm and rest your elbow on the table, holding your hand up by the side of your head.

Pick up the coin in your right hand and start rubbing it into your left elbow. Rub a bit and then drop the coin onto the table. Pick up the coin with your left hand and pretend to place it into your right. Bend your left arm again and as you start to rub with your right hand casually place the coin in your collar with your left hand. Remove your left hand from your collar so that the audience will not become suspicious, then slowly open your right hand and show that the coin has vanished.

The Coin in the Paper

A coin, folded in a piece of paper, vanishes when the paper is torn open.

Use a piece of stiff paper, about 3 by 5 inches. Lay the coin in its center, and fold the paper in half over the coin so that the narrow edges meet. Now make sure the coin is against the fold. Crease the paper down and fold it over once again so that the coin is lifted when you fold the paper, and the ends meet again. You should now have a space between the coin and the fold. In other words you roll the coin in the paper, but not too tightly, as the coin must be able to slide through the "tube" of paper.

Now turn the packet over so that the ends are on top of the bundle. Let someone feel the paper to see that the coin is actually there. Hold the packet vertically in your left hand, and fold the top part down over the top of the coin. Release the pressure on the

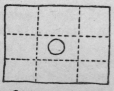

COIN IN CENTER
OF PAPER –
DOTS ARE FOLDS

COIN SLIDING
INTO HAND

coin and let it slip down into your hand. Now fold the bottom part of the bundle up and over the spot where the coin should be.

Take the packet into your right hand, and drop your left hand to your side where you slip the coin into your pocket. Now, with both hands, tear the paper in half, showing the coin is gone. You may reproduce it in a handkerchief, using the method shown in the next trick.

Coin in the Knot

A handkerchief is tied in a knot, and when it is untied by a spectator, a coin is found to be inside.

You may use this method to reproduce a coin which you have made vanish by any of the above methods. Palm a coin in the finger-palm position, and borrow a handkerchief. Allow the coin to slide to the tips of the fingers and hold it with the thumb and finger tips.

Fold the handkerchief by the two opposite corners, and place the coin at one of the corners, beneath the folds, and hold it in place with your thumb. Pull the handkerchief taut, and twirl it so that it becomes like a hollow rope or tube. Bring the corners together and hold them with one hand. Release the pressure on the

COIN FALLS
TO HERE

coin and it will roll into the folds of the handkerchief and stay at the center.

Shake the handkerchief once or twice to be sure the coin is at the loop. Tie a knot, and hand the handkerchief to a spectator to hold. Make a magical pass towards the handkerchief and ask the spectator to untie the knot. He will find the coin inside.

Coin in the Handkerchief

You hold a handkerchief draped over you hand and ask someone to place a coin on it. When you shake out the handkerchief, the coin has vanished.

Double a small rubber band over your fingers and thumb, and place a man's large handkerchief over your hand. Poke a small pocket in the center of the handkerchief to receive the coin. The small well or pocket in the handkerchief will be directly over the palm of your hand and the rubber band will be around, but not touching, the handkerchief. When the coin is dropped on the handkerchief, release the rubber band. This will hold the coin, and when you shake out the handkerchief, the coin will be bundled up in the center of it and will not show.

of a living person on each of the other two slips. Have
the slips folded and dropped into the hat.
When......................from the

4.
Mind-Reading
Tricks

Tricks in which someone apparently reads the mind
of another, or foretells events yet to come have always been popular. The ladies will like this form of
magic especially. You don't need to be psychic to do
these tricks—all you need to know is the secret.

The Name of the Dead

*For this trick, you hand out three slips of paper,
and ask three people to help you. Two are to write the
names of living people on their slip, and the third person, the name of a dead person. These slips are folded
and placed in a hat, without your touching them. You
are then blindfolded, or the hat is held high over your
head so that you cannot see into it. You are able to
reach in and bring out the slip with the dead person's
name.*

This is a very easy trick. Take a sheet of note paper, and tear it into three pieces. The top and bottom
pieces will have one smooth edge and one rough edge,
but the center piece will have two rough edges. Have
someone in the audience write a dead person's name
on the center slip, and two other spectators, the names

of a living person on each of the other two slips. Have the slips folded and dropped into the hat.

When you reach into the hat, all you need to do is feel for the slip with two rough edges. When you have found it, don't bring it out right away. Have the spectators concentrate on the names they have written. Bring out the slip, still folded, and hold it against your head. Build up the suspense until you have created a mystery. Then reveal the slip in your hand as the one with the dead person's name. If you wish, you may leave the room while the names are being written, and be brought in blindfolded for a dramatic presentation.

Famous Names

Have members of the audience call out the names of about ten famous people, living or dead. You write down each name on a separate card. The cards are then well mixed and you make a prediction on a slate. A spectator selects one of the cards. He reads his selection aloud and the name you wrote on the slate is the same as the name read.

You will need ten small cards or a small pad of paper to write the names on, a slate, and a hat.

With everything at hand, ask someone to call out the name of a famous person. Write this down on one of the cards and drop it into the hat. Ask for another name. This time do not write the name that is called, but write the first name that was called. Now both cards in the hat have the same name written on them. As different names are called you continue writing the original name on each card until you have about ten cards in the hat, all with the same name on them. Now write this name on the slate so that the audience does not see it.

Place the slate where it can be seen, but with the writing away from the audience. Invite a spectator to assist you. Shake the hat to mix the cards. Ask the spectator to reach into the hat and select one of the slips, and read the name written on it, aloud. After he does this, turn the slate around to show that the name selected was the same as the one that you predicted on the slate. Be sure and destroy the slips after your performance, so that no one may see them.

The Book Test

You hand a spectator a sealed envelope, and display an ordinary telephone book. You ask the spectator to call out three different digits, which you write down. Another spectator is asked to make certain calculations with the numbers, and announce the result. He is then asked to look in the telephone book at a page and name indicated by the results and read the name at that number. The name in the book is the same as the name in the sealed envelope he has held all along.

Before you start turn to page 108 in the telephone book and count down to the 9th name on the page. Write this name on a slip of paper and seal it in an envelope.

Hand the sealed envelope to a spectator and ask him to hold it. Ask someone to call out three different digits, or have three spectators call out different one-digit numbers. Write this down in plain view, on a slate or large sheet of paper.

Have another spectator come up to make some calculations. For example, suppose the number was 653. Ask him to reverse the number (356), and to subtract the lower number from the higher:

$$\begin{array}{r} 653 \\ 356 \\ \hline 297 \end{array}$$

Ask him now to take the result (297), reverse it, (792) and add the two together:

$$\begin{array}{r} 297 \\ 792 \\ \hline 1089 \end{array}$$

The answer will always be 1089, no matter what numbers are used. If only two figures result from the subtraction, be sure to add a zero at the left, such as 079.

Now ask the spectator with the telephone book to look on the page indicated by the first three numbers, 108, and to count down to the name indicated by the last number, 9. Ask him to read aloud the name that appears at that position. Have the spectator with the envelope open your prediction, which proves to be correct.

If you wish, you may use this as a telepathy stunt instead of a prediction stunt. In that case, do not write a prediction, but ask the spectator who is looking in the telephone book to concentrate on the name. With great concentration, and drama, tell him the name he is looking at. Of course you have memorized it before the start of the trick. To vary the program, use a dictionary, or book instead of a phone book.

The Magic Numbers

You write a prediction on a slate and cover it with a handkerchief. You then pass out a pad of paper to a spectator and ask him to write a four digit number on the pad. Two other spectators each write a four digit number under the first. Have a fourth spectator add them together and announce the result. The slate is uncovered and there on the slate is the answer.

Use a pad about 5 by 7 inches with a cover. The pad should open at the narrow edge (top). On the first page write down a four digit number, and under this two more four digit numbers just as if they were to be added together. When writing your figures, try and make them look as if they were written by different people. Draw a line under the row of figures so they may be added together. On another sheet of paper add these figures. Do not write them on the first page, but memorize the total, or write it very faintly on the slate. Fold back the cover and first page of the pad (with the figures) so that the second (blank) page is in view.

To start the trick, show the slate and appear to concentrate. Write down the total of the figures you wrote on page one, on the slate, so that no one can see them. Cover the slate with a handkerchief and give it to someone to hold, or stand it up in plain view.

Go to one of the spectators and ask him to write a four digit number on the pad. Hold the cover and first page down along the back of the pad so that he writes on the second page. Repeat this with two more spectators from different parts of the room so that you are walking about quite a bit. Ask the third person who writes down figures to draw a line under the column of figures so that they may be added.

Now walk to the other side of the audience, and as

you do so, fold the top page over onto the pad, so that *your* figures are on top. As you do this, tear out your page, close the cover of the pad, and ask a spectator to add the figures. Give him the pad to rest the sheet of paper on. Ask him to announce the result after he has added the figures. Have the first spectator, who is holding the slate, uncover it and read what is written on it. The totals will agree.

Prediction

You are able to predict the total of some numbers you could not have known at the beginning of the trick.

You will need an "assistant" or "stooge" for this one, but it is worth letting someone in on this, because of the result of the trick. Explain the trick to him in advance so he will know what he needs to do.

On a small piece of paper, write down your prediction. Any four digit number over 6,000 will do. Fold your prediction, and place it in a sealed envelope which will be in view of the audience all through the trick.

During the trick, ask a spectator the year in which he was born. Suppose he says 1920. Write this on a large slate. Ask another spectator to name a date that is important historically such as: 1914. Write this below the first figure. Ask another spectator what year was important in his life. Suppose he says 1941. Write that down under the other figures. Stress to the audience that there is no possible way for you to know the dates these people would choose. Now tell them to make it more difficult you will have another number added, about which you know nothing and which you will not see. Go to your "assistant" and hand him the slate, and tell him to write any number under the three others and add them all together. When he has finished, ask him to read the total aloud. Ask someone to open the envelope you placed on your table before the start of the show, and to read what it says. It will have the same total as the one just read.

Now for a little more explanation. Your assistant must know the total you have predicted. He must add a number which will give the total you have predicted. In other words, he holds a slate that shows the following.

1920	(Year of birth)
1914	(Historical year)
1941	(Year of importance)
- - -	(The number he must add)
8477	(Your prediction)

He must add 2702 to make the correct total. This is a very clever trick, and don't pass it up because it requires a secret assistant. The effect on the audience is what counts, not how simple a trick may seem to you.

The Same as You

This is a gag which you can use to get a laugh.

Hand a spectator a slip of paper and tell him to go to the other side of the room and write a short sentence on the paper, fold it and hand it to another spectator. Appear to concentrate very deeply, and say, "I will write the same as you on my slip," which you do. Hand your slip to the spectator who is holding the other slip. Ask him to open the spectator's slip and read it aloud. Now you say, "That's right. I wrote the same as you." And that's exactly what you *have* written—just the four words "The same as you!"

You may vary this by writing, "That's right!" on a slip. Proceed as above. Have the spectator's slip read aloud, and then ask him to read your slip. Of course, he will say, "That's right."

Book Trick

You show a book, a novel, textbook, or any kind of book, and have a spectator insert a card anywhere he chooses. The book is opened at the page indicated by the card, and you are able to tell what is on that page, either by a written prediction, or by saying it aloud.

Use a book with a plain cover. Choose a page near the center and write down the first sentence on a slip of paper or memorize it. Place a card about halfway into the book at this page.

Pick up the book, but hide the projecting card as you go to a spectator and hand him a plain card. Have him thrust the card into the book anywhere he wishes. Now, if you planned to use a written prediction, hand it to another spectator to hold. As you move about turn the book over, revealing the end from which your card projects.

If you don't use a written predicition, turn the book around as you approach another spectator and have him open the book to the page indicated by the card. Be sure to cover the card that still projects from the other end with your hand. As you hand the spectator the book, slip the card out of the book, without letting him see you do this. As the spectator holds the book, ask him to concentrate on the first line on the page that is indicated by the card. Then tell him what it says, or have him read it aloud and then read your prediction. Don't merely tell him that the page says so-and-so, but appear to concentrate deeply and state the sentence slowly and mysteriously.

The Mysterious Numbers

Here's a trick you can use to fool and amuse yourself, as well as others.

Think of a small number. Now double it, add 4, divide by 2. Subtract the number you first thought of. Your answer is 2. Right?

This works automatically. For instance, say your first number was 3. Doubled, it becomes 6, add 4 and you get 10. Divide by 2, equals 5; subtract the number you first thought of (3) and your answer will be 2.

When you do this, the answer will always be one half of the number you add. When you repeat this, change the number you tell people to add so that the answer will be different. Remember, if you tell them to add 10, their answer will be 5 — always one half of the number they add. Try it!

5.
Rope, String and Ribbon Tricks

The Rope Release

This is a Houdini-type trick in which you escape. You will need a handkerchief and a piece of clothesline about 6 feet long.

Have a spectator tie your wrists together by tying each wrist with an end of the handkerchief. Put your hands together, but don't cross them.

Now have him pass the rope between your wrists, and pull the rope so that its center is between your wrists, while he holds the ends. Tell him to hold the ends tightly so you cannot escape.

Turn away from the audience, and as you do this, get a hold on the rope and pass a loop of this through the circle of the handkerchief around your right wrist.

Push this loop through from the inside, out towards your hands. Pull the loop up to the front, pass it over your hand and down the back of your hand. A slight tug will pull it out of the handkerchief at the back of your hand, and you will be free.

Hold the rope for a moment as you turn back to the audience. The audience sees the spectator still holding the ends of the rope, and your wrists still securely tied. Then drop the rope on the floor. This sounds quite simple, but it is really very baffling to the audience.

A Piece of String

You show a piece of brown twine and have a spectator cut it in two. You hold the pieces far apart so that the audience can see clearly that the pieces are actually cut. By making a magic pass the string is restored.

You need a length of ordinary brown wrapping twine and some beeswax, sometimes called "magician's wax."

Beforehand taper each end of the twine to a point with sharp scissors or a knife, and apply a daub of wax to each end. When rubbed well, the wax will become soft, and it may be easily worked into the twine.

Now show the string, and have a spectator cut it in half with a pair of scissors while you hold the ends. Hold your hands far apart, one piece in each hand so that the audience can clearly see that you have two pieces. Switch the twine from hand to hand so that you end up with the waxed end of each up, one piece in each hand.

Now bring your hands together so that the waxed ends meet, and allow them to overlap. Squeeze the ends together tightly and roll them together between your thumb and fingers. This will cement the ends together because of the wax. Now take one of the free ends and hold it up next to the waxed ends, and pretend you are going to tie a knot. Say: "Most people would tie the pieces together, but a magician just drops the center and the string is restored." Let the center drop, still holding the one end in your hand and show that the string is restored.

Walking Through a Rope

You tie a spectator with two lengths of rope. You and someone from the audience hold the ends of these ropes. As you pronounce some magic words, the spectator walks through the ropes and is free.

In advance, get two pieces of soft rope about 6 or more feet in length. Lay the ropes together on a table, and tie a piece of thin white cotton thread around both ropes in their centers. Roll the two ropes as one, into a neat bundle. Now your trick is ready to perform.

Ask two spectators to come up and help you. Unroll the two ropes, and hold them up by the ends.

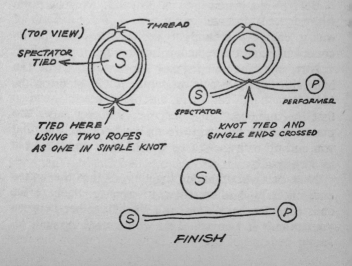

Have the first spectator stand at the center of your stage, and the second at the far side. Hand the ends of two of the ropes to the second spectator while you hold the other ends, without letting him see the thread in the centers. Ask him to pull to see if the ropes are strong and then drop his ends.

Take the ropes by their centers, your hand hiding the thread, and walk behind the spectator in the middle of the stage. Hold the ropes by the centers, at the back, and slightly separate them, but do not break the thread. Apparently, bring the ends of both ropes around from the back to the front of the spectator. What you actually do is to bring the two ends of the same rope around one side and the two ends of the other rope around the other side of the spectator.

Now tie a half-knot in front of the spectator using both ropes as one. Have the other spectator hold one set of ends and you hold the other set with the tied spectator between you.

Ask the spectator holding the ropes to drop either one of his ends, and you drop one of your ends. It doesn't matter which end is dropped. Now take the two dropped ends and simply cross—do not tie—them, giving one of your ends to the spectator and taking one of his. Tell the spectator holding the ropes to hold tightly, and when you signal him, to pull hard. The spectator who is tied is to step back two steps on the signal.

Give the signal, and pull on your two ends. The rope will seem to penetrate the body of the spectator and he will be free. The ropes will hang down in front of him held by you and the other spectator. What happens is that when you pull, the thread breaks, and the ropes merely slide around the spectator's body. Have the spectators look over the ropes. Be sure to ask the spectator if it hurt when the ropes went through his body!

Ring on the String

You are able to place a solid ring on a string while the ends of it are in full view of the audience.

Use a piece of string about 3 feet long and stretch it out on a table. Make a loop on the string and place a safety pin through both sides of the loop. Borrow a finger ring and lay it on the table next to the loop. Now, place a handkerchief over the ring and string, leaving the ends of the string in view.

Put your hands under the handkerchief and open the pin; release one side of the loop and close the pin again. Take the ring, and thread it over the safety pin and enclose the other side of the original loop in the pin. Place your index finger in the new loop formed by the ring and take your other hand out from under the handkerchief.

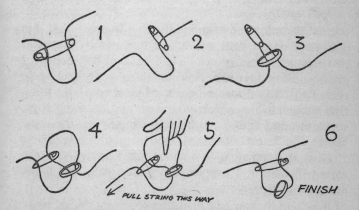

Take the end of the string on the side nearest your uncovered hand, and pull it so that the other end goes under the handkerchief and out on the other side. Be sure and hold your finger securely in the loop as the string is pulled, as this action threads the ring onto the string. In other words, the loop must pull through your finger easily, so that it does not stop the action of pulling on the string. Now show how it is impossible to remove the ring without opening the safety pin and sliding the ring off the end.

The Ring on the Rope

A large ring or bracelet is examined by the audience, and your wrists are tied together with a piece of rope. The ring is handed to you and you turn your back for a moment. When you turn around, the ring is on the rope. The rope must be untied to release the ring.

You will need a 3-foot length of rope, and two duplicate rings or bracelets large enough to slip over your hand easily.

Before you start, slip one of the rings over your left wrist and slide it up your arm under your coat sleeve out of sight.

Let the audience examine the ring to prove that it is ordinary. Have your wrists tied together by a spectator, leaving about a foot or two of rope between your wrists. Then take the ring and turn your back. Slip this ring into an inside pocket of your coat and bring the duplicate ring down your arm and onto the rope. Turn around and show the ring securely on the rope. Have the knots examined, and also the ring. Show that it is impossible to remove the ring without untying the knots. Have someone untie you, and thank him for helping you.

The Ring Release

Thread a ring on a string. Two spectators hold the ends of it and when a handkerchief is thrown over the ring, you are able to remove the ring!

You can use two duplicate rings (finger ring size) or two skeleton type keys, or two Chinese coins with holes in their centers.

We will suppose you use the rings, although the action is the same for the coins or keys. Beforehand place one ring in your left coat pocket. Have a spectator examine the other ring and string. Ask him to thread the ring on the string, hold one end, and give the other end to another spectator to hold. Throw a handkerchief over the ring and string, and as you do this, remove the other ring from your pocket, in the finger-palm position, page 3. Place both hands under the handkerchief and ask the spectators to hold tightly to their ends of the string but to give you some slack.

Take the duplicate ring and push a loop of string through its center, and loop it over the top so that it will stay on the string. At first glance it will look as if it were threaded. Place your right hand over the ring that is actually on the string and tell one spectator it is

LOOP AROUND
DUPLICATE RING

RING ON STRING
(SLIDE OFF)

necessary to swing the string back and forth. Slide your right hand to the end of the string and take the end from the spectator for just a moment to show him how to swing the string. Hand it back to him, and as you do, slide the ring off the end of the string and you can put it in your pocket. Remove the handkerchief, and say you thought they might like to see the trick done without the handkerchief. Place your hand over the ring as you remove the handkerchief with the other hand. Take the loop off and the ring will appear to melt right through the string. Let the spectators examine the ring and string once again.

Cut and Restored Twine

By the use of a magic ring a piece of twine is restored after having been cut in two.

Take a 3-foot piece of twine or wrapping cord and lay it out on a table. Separate the strands of string in the center and pull them out in a direction perpendicular to the twine. Twist them so they look like the ends of the twine. Now pick up the string by the middle and pull the two twisted strands so they look like the real ends. Wax the real ends as you did in the trick "A Piece of String," page 42. Roll the ends together so that they look like the middle of the string. What you have done now is to make the center look like the ends and the ends like the center.

To begin the trick, hold the string by the fake ends (those you have pulled out from the center) in your left hand, your thumb and fingers hiding the joint. Let the waxed "center" hang down. Have a spectator cut the part that hangs down with a pair of scissors, right through both pieces at once. Put the cut piece in your pocket so no one can see the waxed ends.

Bring out your "magic finger ring" any ring will do, and thread it over one of the cut ends, drawing it up

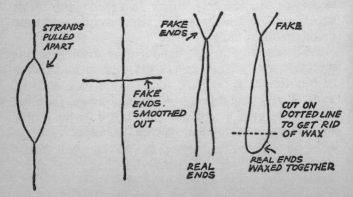

to the twisted end in your hand. Lay the ring and twisted ends in your left palm and close your hand over them. Have a spectator hold one cut end in each hand. Say that if you opened your hand the ring would fall, but he is to pull gently, but firmly on each end. As he does so, run your hand, with the ring, back and forth along the string to flatten the strands. Remove your hand, and show that the string is restored and the ring is hanging on it.

Cut and Restored Rope or String

A rope or string is cut in two, and restored.

Use a piece of rope or string about 3 feet long. Cut a 3- or 4-inch piece from one end. Loop this small piece, and place it in your left hand in the finger-palm position, with the loop part towards your fingers.

When you are ready to start the trick, with the small loop in your hand, hold up the large piece, one end in each hand. Now take the center of the rope in your right hand and place it in your left with the ends hanging down. You will seem to pull up the center of the rope through your left fist with your right hand, but you really pull up the small loop so that it appears to be the center of the long piece. The real center of the long piece will be held by your third and fourth left fingers, while the small piece is held by your thumb and first finger.

With your right hand, hand a pair of scissors to a spectator and ask him to cut the rope in half. After he has done this, take the scissors from him and cut away all remaining pieces of the small loop. Take the rope by the ends, one in each hand, and let the center swing down, showing that the rope is restored.

The Ring in the Knot

A large ring is thrown into a knot while the ends of a piece of rope are held in your hands.

Make a single, simple, large loose knot in a piece of rope about 4 feet in length. The knot should be in the center of the rope, while one end is held in each hand. The loop formed by the knot in the center of the rope should be larger than the ring you use.

Use a fairly large ring or bracelet and let the spectators examine it. Pick up the ring in one hand, and say that you are going to try to hang it on the rope. You are still holding the ends of the rope, one end in each hand. Make a throwing motion at the knot with the ring. As you do this, slip the end of the rope in your hand through the ring without letting anyone see you do it. Just keep your fingers closed over the ring and rope. When you actually throw the ring, be sure it goes through the loop of the knot. Now, when you pull on the ends of the rope, the ring will be tied on the rope.

This requires a little practice, but if you make the knot large enough it will work easily.

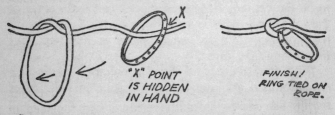

"X" POINT IS HIDDEN IN HAND

RING THROWN "INTO" LOOP

FINISH! RING TIED ON ROPE.

Escape

Your wrists are tied tightly behind your back, but you are able to escape almost instantly, or you may appear to be free, but when the knots are examined, you seem to be securely tied.

Have two spectators come up to assist you. Have one stand on your right and one on your left. Face the audience and extend your left arm, palm up in front of you. Have one of the spectators tie your left wrist securely in the center of the rope with a tight square

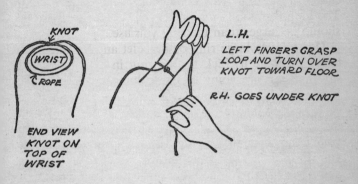

KNOT

WRIST

ROPE

END VIEW
KNOT ON
TOP OF
WRIST

L.H.
LEFT FINGERS GRASP
LOOP AND TURN OVER
KNOT TOWARD FLOOR

R.H. GOES UNDER KNOT

(double) knot. This will leave the ends of the rope hanging down.

Now place your hands behind your back and as you do this, pick up a loop of slack with your left fingers. Hold this securely between your wrists, by placing your right wrist under the knot on your left wrist. This is all done very quickly. Now turn your back to the audience, and have the ends of the rope brought up over top of your right wrist and tied tightly.

It now appears as if you are tightly tied. Turn around and face the audience. You will find that your right wrist can be instantly released and replaced in the loop of slack.

When you replace your hand in the loop, bend your left fingers inward, pick up the slack, give it a twist and place it against your left wrist. Now press your wrists together, and hold the rope in place.

After you have been tied, stand facing the audience

between your two assistants. Have them stand close to
you. Release your right hand from the loop, and reach
out and touch the spectator on your right, on his *right*
shoulder. He will turn around, and of course the audience will see your hand and laugh. As soon as you
have tapped him on the shoulder, replace your hand
in the loop and turn around and show that you are
still securely tied. Repeat this one or two times, and
then walk over to the right side of the other spectator
and repeat this with him. Always show your hands
tied after you have tapped one of the spectators.

To end the trick, either have your hands untied by
the spectators, or release yourself. I think it is better
to have yourself untied as it makes the trick more
mysterious.

The best kind of rope to use for this trick is a piece
of sash cord about three or four feet long. You should
handle it before doing this trick so that it will become
soft and pliable.

The Bagged Ring

*You borrow a ring and cause it to vanish. Then
push a pencil through the sides of a paper bag and the
ring is discovered on the pencil.*

Take a cheap ring and place it in the corner of a
heavy handkerchief. Sew a small square of material
that matches the handkerchief over the ring so that a
closed pocket is formed, concealing the ring. Have a
small paper bag of thin paper lying on your table with
its end open. Have a long pencil in your outside coat
pocket.

Borrrow a ring from the audience, and place it under the special handkerchief. Get the corner with the
sewn-in ring under the center of the handkerchief and
let a spectator hold this. He will think he is holding
the borrowed ring. As you remove your hand from

under the handkerchief, keep the borrowed ring in your hand concealing it from view.

Pick up the paper bag with the hand that holds the ring. Put your fingers inside the bag with the ring, but keep your thumb on the outside. With the ring between your fingers and the side of the bag you can let the audience look into the bag and see that it is empty.

Take the pencil in the other hand and push it through the side nearest the ring, at about the center of the bag, and get the ring on the pencil. Continue pushing the pencil through the bag so that it comes out on the other side of it. Have a spectator hold one end of the pencil in each hand, with the bag hanging down between the ends of the pencil. Close the bag by twisting its top.

Now grasp the handkerchief by one corner and whip it from the spectator's hand. Shake it to show that the ring has vanished. Go over to the spectator who is holding the bag and pencil and grasp the bag by its bottom. Pull it quickly downward, tearing the paper away from the pencil. The ring will be found hanging on the pencil while the spectator still holds the ends of the pencil. Return the ring to its owner.

Magic Hair Ribbon

A hair ribbon is cut into several pieces, and these are dropped to prove the ribbon is really cut. You then restore it.

Use a fairly heavy ribbon, a yard or more in length, and 1 inch or more wide. Cut off about 5 inches from one end. Pin this short piece to the center of the long piece with straight pins. Use one pin at each end of the short piece. It will look like the original ribbon when it is held up, and the piece won't show.

To begin the trick, take the ribbon by its center and

draw it up through your closed left fist by its center. As you do this, the short piece will buckle. That is the piece that you pull out of the top of your fist. The audience, of course, believes the short piece they see is the center of the long ribbon. (This is similar to the trick, "Cut and Restored Rope or String," page 49).

Cut in half the short loop of ribbon that sticks up from your fist. Cut it several more times, letting the small pieces drop. Continue cutting until the short piece is cut down to the pins. Pretend to adjust the ribbon, and pull out the pins—just let them drop on the floor, unnoticed.

Now all you need to do is reach down with your right hand and grasp one of the ends of the long ribbon. Let the center of the ribbon drop out of your left fist, and the ribbon will hang down, completely restored.

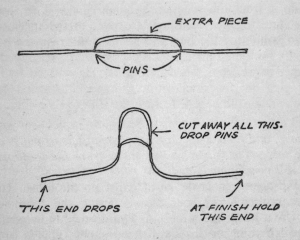

EXTRA PIECE

PINS

CUT AWAY ALL THIS.
DROP PINS

THIS END DROPS

AT FINISH HOLD
THIS END

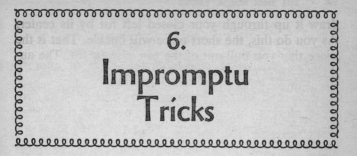

6.
Impromptu Tricks

These tricks look impromptu. They are called "close-up" tricks, because they are good for small groups. They will all seem to be done on the spur of the moment, without active beforehand preparation. You might also call them "pocket tricks" because the items you will use for them can all be carried in your pocket. These tricks are good when a group of friends are sitting around and someone says, "Show us a trick."

The Magnetic Toothpick

You rub the end of a wooden toothpick on your sleeve, and hold it close to some small bits of paper on the table. The paper will fly away from the toothpick as if it were magnetized.

Put a few small scraps of paper on the table. Rub the toothpick on your sleeve. Bring the toothpick slowly towards the paper. As you do this, blow gently through your mouth towards the paper. This is what makes the paper move. No one must see you blow, of course. Anyone else who tries to do this trick won't be able to "magnetize" the toothpick. Instead of a toothpick, you could use a pencil.

The Electric Toothpicks

When you bring one toothpick close to another one, one of them will fly up into the air.

Place one of the toothpicks on the edge of the table, so that part of it sticks out over the edge. Rub the other toothpick on your sleeve and bring it up under the toothpick on the table. The one on the table will jump into the air as you barely touch its end. In doing this, you must get the nail of your second finger under the end of the toothpick in your hand and give it a slight "flick" as you touch the ends of the toothpicks together.

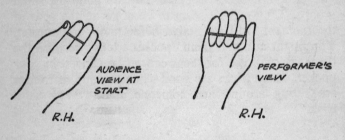

AUDIENCE
VIEW AT
START

R.H.

PERFORMER'S
VIEW

R.H.

The Jumping Rubber Band

You place a rubber band around your first and second fingers and it will jump to your third and fourth fingers.

Let everyone see that the rubber band is really around your first two fingers. Pull at the band with the thumb and forefinger of your other hand. Pull first from the front and then from the back. On the third pull, from the front, before you let the band snap back, close your hand so that all four fingers are inside the band. From the front it will look as if it were only around the first two fingers. Now open your hand and the band will be snapped very quickly around your third and fourth fingers, leaving your first two fingers free.

When doing this trick, use a fairly large rubber band, one that is loose on your fingers. It will be easier for you to slip all your fingers into it.

The Magic Safety Pins

Get a spectator to link two safety pins together. The trick is to separate them by pulling them apart without opening either one.

Take the pins from the spectator, and hold one pin in your left hand with your thumb and forefinger, by the small end, with the opening of the pin facing upward. Turn the other pin around the end so it hangs from the upper bar of the left hand pin, small end at the top, both sides over the lower bar, and the left side over the upper bar. The pins should form an X.

With the pins in this position, hold them tightly and pull your hands apart quickly. The pin moving to the right will slip through the catch of the other pin without forcing it to spring open.

A large blanket pin is the best size to use.

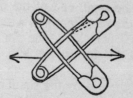

The Rubber Pencil

You hold a pencil between your fingers and it bends as if it were made of rubber.

Hold an ordinary lead pencil with the thumb and forefinger of your right hand, about a third of the distance from the end. Hold it horizontally with the longer part of the pencil pointing towards the left. Hold it very loosely and move your hand up and down in short, quick strokes, letting it move somewhat like a seesaw. The pencil will seem flexible enough to be bending in your fingers.

Handkerchief and Safety Pin

Take a safety pin and pin it through the edge of a handkerchief. Get two spectators to hold up the handkerchief. If you know the secret, you can pull the pin back and forth along the handkerchief without damaging it.

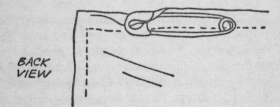

BACK
VIEW

Get two spectators to hold up a handkerchief. Take the safety pin and pin it through the handkerchief near the edge. The small end of the pin should be on the top edge of the handkerchief, with the head of the pin above it. The open side of the pin should be to the right, and the solid side to the left, completely over the edge.

Take hold of the pin by the small end and move it almost parallel to the upper edge of the handkerchief. Pull the pin quickly, but steadily to the right. The pin will seem to be running through the material but you will really be folding the material over through the catch of the pin. It will sound as if the handkerchief were being ripped. When you stop moving the pin, it will still be through the handkerchief, but the cloth will be undamaged. Be sure to always use a heavy handkerchief. Practice with scraps of cloth until you get the feel of the trick.

Whose Button?

You apparently pull a button off a spectator's coat or vest, and cause it to sew itself back on.

Place three buttons which would match a man's coat or vest in your left hand coat pocket. A black, brown, and gray button will do.

Find a spectator whose coat buttons match one of those you have in your pocket. (Vest buttons are easier to handle, but sometimes it is difficult to find a man with a vest.)

Ask him to step forward, and with the correct color button in your left hand, unbutton his coat. Place your right hand under the cloth of the coat, and your left thumb over the lower half of his coat button. Get the loose button, hidden from view, under your left thumb. Pull at the man's button with your right hand a few times covering the button for an instant. With your fingers under the coat, slide your left thumb upward, causing the loose button to come into view and hiding his button.

With your right hand, you apparently pull off his button—actually it is the loose one—and hold it up for him to see. Before he realizes what has happened, finger-palm (page 3) the button in your right hand. Wave your right hand at his coat, and moving your left thumb off of his button, show that it has restored itself. Drop the extra button into your right-hand coat pocket.

Swami

A weight on the end of a string, held by a spectator, swings back and forth in answer to the questions addressed to it.

Use a spool, a light fishing sinker, a rubber ball, or even a stone. Tie or tack a 12-inch length of string to the weight. On the other end of the string, tie a ring about 1½ inches in diameter, or tie a loop of the same size in the end of the string.

Hand this "Swami" to a spectator, and have him place his right forefinger in the loop and hang the weight in front of him. Tell him to keep his finger extended, as if pointing, and to hold it very still. You are going to ask him some questions. He is not to answer, but Swami will, by causing the weight to swing to and fro for a "yes" answer, and in a circle for a "no" answer.

Ask him several simple questions that can be answered with a yes or no. No matter how hard he tries to keep his hand still, the weight will move and answer his question.

Why does it work? I don't know, but it does! Try it!

Crazy Money

You roll a five dollar and a one dollar bill around a pencil and make them change places.

Borrow a five dollar bill and lay it face-up, flat on the table. Borrow a one dollar bill and lay it face-up on top of the five. Call attention to the fact that the one dollar bill is on top of the five.

Now lay a pencil across the narrow end of both bills, and start rolling the pencil with the bills around it. When you come to the end of the bills the five will "flop over." Stop rolling at this point and begin rolling the pencil backwards, or towards you. The one dollar bill will be rolled under the pencil. When you have finished unrolling the bills, the five dollar bill will be on top of the one dollar bill.

The Thread and the Straw

Run a threaded needle through a drinking straw. The ends of the thread should be held by two spectators. Cut the straw in two with a pair of scissors and the thread will not be harmed.

Before you start, make a slit about 1½ inches long in the center of the straw, lengthwise, with a razor blade. Hold the straw, and have a spectator push the needle through it, pulling the thread through the straw. Have each end of the thread held by spectators. Bend the ends of the straw slightly downwards above the slit which must face *towards* the floor. This pulls the straw away from the thread. The thread will be underneath the straw. Insert your scissors between the straw and thread, scissors above the thread. Cut through the straw, and you will appear to be cutting the thread as well. Separate the pieces of straw, and let them hang on the thread showing that the thread is unharmed.

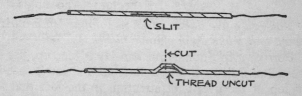

What Dollar?

You borrow a dollar bill from someone in the audience, then throw it to another spectator. Without looking at the bill you are able to tell its serial number!

Memorize the serial number of a dollar bill and crumple it up into a ball. Place it in your right-hand coat pocket.

Ask someone to lend you a dollar. Tell him to crumple the bill into a small ball, so that he can toss it to you. As you are talking to him, place your right hand in your pocket and get the bill you have hidden. Hold it in the crotch of your thumb on the palm side of your hand.

Catch the dollar bill from someone in the audience in both hands, and get it into your left hand in the finger-palm position (page 3). Bring the bill you had in your right hand into view and look toward the opposite side of the audience from which the bill was thrown. Toss it to someone there and ask him to unfold the bill and look at the serial number. Meanwhile put the dollar bill from your left hand—the one that was thrown to you—into your pocket.

Appear to concentrate deeply and call off the serial number you memorized very slowly and with much effort. Have the spectator who holds the bill verify the number. It looks as if you have read the number of the borrowed bill. Ask the person in the audience who loaned you the bill to raise his hand. Look at him, while pointing towards the spectator who holds the bill, and say, "The gentleman over there owes you a dollar!" This gets a laugh. Have the bill returned to the rightful owner.

The Broken Toothpick

You wrap a toothpick in a handkerchief and get a spectator to break it. When you unwrap the handkerchief, the toothpick falls out unharmed.

Beforehand, take a handkerchief with a fairly wide

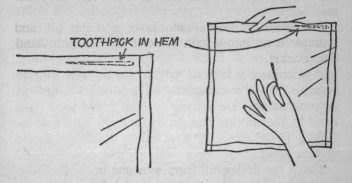

TOOTHPICK IN HEM

hem and force a wooden toothpick into the hem where it won't show.

Show another toothpick to the audience and place it in the center of the handkerchief. Wrap it up very carefully, and ask a spectator to feel it through the handkerchief. What he feels is the toothpick in the hem, because you have folded that corner of the handkerchief up under its center. Be sure not to let the loose toothpick fall out.

Ask the spectator to break it in two. (He, of course, breaks the one in the hem.) The audience can hear it snap. After making several passes over the handkerchief, flick it open and let the real toothpick drop out—unharmed.

Thimble Vanish

You place a thimble on your right forefinger and then pretend to throw the thimble up in the air, and it will vanish.

Practice this move, because it is the basis of all thimble tricks. Place the thimble on your right forefinger. Bend down your finger, so the thimble is gripped in the fork of the thumb and forefinger. It is left there, and you extend your finger, holding all of your fingers apart. Your hand will appear empty. The thimble is held the same way that you held the dollar bill in the "What Dollar?" trick (page 61).

Now bend your forefinger down again and pick up the thimble on it. If these motions are done quickly, and your hand is kept in motion, the thimble will appear to vanish and reappear right before the eyes of your audience.

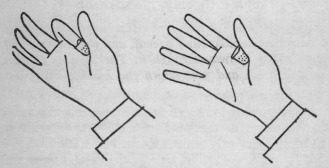

To do the "Throw-Vanish" trick, start with the thimble on your right forefinger, the back of your hand towards the audience. Make a throwing motion upward. The eyes of the audience, as well as yours, follow the imaginary flight of the thimble. As you make the motion, the thimble is quickly "thumb-palmed," as described above. The thimble has vanished. You may reproduce it from anywhere you wish, by quickly reaching behind your left elbow, under the table, or from anywhere you desire.

Another Thimble Vanish

Another method to vanish the thimble is to appear to take the thimble from your right finger with the left hand.

Bring your left hand over the extended right fingers. It will cover your right fingers for a moment.

While they are covered, you quickly thumb-palm the thimble in your right hand, and wrap your left hand around your right forefinger as if to pull off the thimble. Your right hand will appear to be empty. Open your left hand and show that the thimble has vanished. Produce it from wherever you desire.

Thimble Through Handkerchief

You place a thimble on your forefinger, then place a borrowed handkerchief over it, and the thimble will seem to go halfway through it. The thimble is then pushed back, and you return the handkerchief, undamaged.

For this trick you will need two thimbles. One must fit loosely over the other. Use plastic thimbles, and cut away the lower part of the larger one, saving only the tip. When you place this thimble tip on top of the smaller one, it will not show, even at a short distance.

To begin the trick, place the thimble, with the extra tip on it, in your left fist. Now place your right forefinger into your left fist and slip the thimble on it, but leave the extra tip in your left hand.

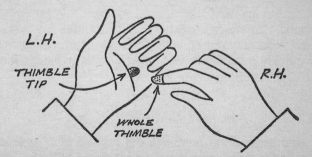

Hold your right forefinger upward and place the handkerchief over the top of it. Stroke your right forefinger with your left hand (over the top of the cloth).

Get the false tip into the thumb-palm position (page 64) and as you stroke your forefinger bring the false tip over the top of the right forefinger, and force it over the top of the cloth. It will now look as if the thimble has gone halfway through the cloth. Repeat the stroking business, and then remove the false tip in the crotch of your left thumb.

Now, using your left hand, pull the handkerchief off your right hand, and show the thimble on your right forefinger. Now you must appear to pull off the thimble into your left hand, and as you do so, get the false tip back onto the thimble, and show that both hands are empty, except for the thimble.

7.
After-Dinner Tricks

The tricks in this chapter are designed for you to do after dinner, right at the table. All the things you will need are found at the table, or in the pockets of your audience.

The Vanishing Sugar

You vanish a lump of sugar and cause it to pass right through the table.

Secretly get a lump of paper-wrapped sugar, the kind you find in most restaurants, and carefully unwrap it, so the paper remains intact. Close up the end of the paper so it looks as if it still contained sugar. Place the piece of real sugar in your lap.

Show the paper and handle it as if it were a real lump of sugar. Place this make-believe piece of sugar on the table. Call attention to it. Raise your right hand above the paper, and bring your palm down sharply on the table and flatten the paper. Let your audience see that the sugar is gone. Then reach under the table with your left hand, and get the piece of real sugar out of your lap. Lay it on the table, showing that the sugar has apparently penetrated the table.

The Magic Knife

You pick up a small butter knife and place specks of paper on its blade. The spots vanish, appear, and jump on and off the knife.

Slightly moisten two small pieces of paper napkin or newspaper. Stick these to one side of the blade of the knife, about an inch apart.

Hold the knife between the thumb and index finger of your right hand. The following is called the "Paddle-Move," and although it may sound difficult it is really very easy to do. What you do is to appear to show both sides of the knife while actually you show only one.

With the tip of your right thumb on the right edge of the handle, and the tip of your forefinger on the left edge of the handle, the blade of the knife should point to the right as it is held horizontally. Your palm should be facing slightly upward.

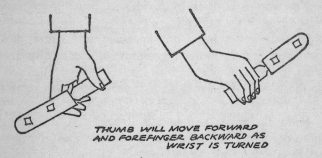

THUMB WILL MOVE FORWARD AND FOREFINGER BACKWARD AS WRIST IS TURNED

You will seem to show the other side of the knife if you turn the knife over so that your palm faces downward. Move the tip of your thumb forward, and the tip of your forefinger backward, turning the knife over between your thumb and forefinger. This turnover is done at the same time you turn your hand over. You must practice this motion.

Show the knife (which really has two spots on only one side) spot-side up and call attention to the fact that it has spots on one side (pretend to turn it over using the method described above) and spots on the other side. Now place your left hand over and around the blade of the knife, spot-side up, and pretend to wipe the spots off. What you really do is to turn the knife over under cover of your hand. Using the same method you can show that both sides are blank. Be sure to show your audience that your left hand is empty. Now place your left hand over the knife again, and show that the spots have come back.

Then remove one of the spots, and show how the spot from the other side vanishes also. You will apparently have only one spot on each side. Now remove the last spot, and by turning the knife over, you can show that the spot on the other side has also vanished. Place the knife on the table, so that anyone who cares to, may examine it.

The Vanishing Salt Shaker

You cause a salt shaker, covered with a sheet of paper, to penetrate the table.

Place a coin on the table in front of you. Place a salt shaker on top of it. Tell everyone to watch the coin as you are going to cause it to do something very

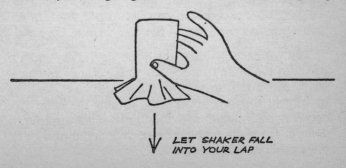

LET SHAKER FALL
INTO YOUR LAP

strange. Say that since the shaker is made of glass, the audience can still see through it.

Now take a sheet of paper and bend it around the salt shaker, so that the paper retains the shape of the shaker. Pick up the shaker with the paper around it, and tell everyone to watch the coin. Cover the coin again with the paper-covered shaker, tapping the glass of the shaker against the coin so that it makes a noise.

Lift the shaker once again, calling attention to the coin, and bring the shaker to the edge of the table, and let it fall into your lap. Place the paper (which still looks as if it holds the shaker) over the coin again. Raise your hand above it, and bring your hand down on the paper, crushing it flat. Pick up the paper and apologize, because the coin is still there. Tell your audience that you made a mistake and made the *salt shaker* go through the table! Reach into your lap and bring the shaker up and place it on the table.

The Sugar Tells

You print the initials of a spectator on a lump of sugar. The sugar is then dissolved, but the initials are found on the spectator's hand.

Ask a spectator what his initials are, and print them on the wide surface of a lump of sugar. Use a pencil with a soft lead or pen with indelible ink. After you have written the initials, secretly press your right thumb down hard on top of the initials, and they will be printed on it.

Drop the sugar into a glass of water with initials face-up so they may be seen. Take the spectator's right hand in your right hand, his palm down, your thumb (with the imprint) next to his palm, and your fingers over the back of his hand. Ask him to place his hand, palm down, over the mouth of the glass. Press your thumb slightly against his palm and transfer the initials to his hand.

Tell everyone to watch the initials disappear from the sugar, as the sugar dissolves. When the letters are gone from the sugar, ask the spectator to turn his hand over, and he will find that the initials have transferred themselves from the sugar to his hand.

The Paper Napkin Ball

You make some small paper balls from a paper napkin. They multiply, vanish, and reappear in a surprising way.

Before you start, place a small paper ball made from ⅓ of a paper napkin into your right coat pocket, along with a quarter. When you are ready to start the trick take a fresh paper napkin and, in front of your audience, tear it into three parts. Roll each part into a paper ball, and place them on the table.

To start just ask someone how many balls he sees and as you talk, casually reach in your pocket and get

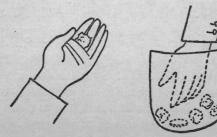

the extra ball in your right hand in the finger-palm position (page 3). Your right hand is palm-down on the table and your left hand palm-up. Reach over with your right hand and pick up a ball with your thumb and forefinger. Place it into your left hand and say, "One." Pick up another ball and place it, along with the palmed ball, in your left hand saying, "Two." Quickly close your left hand. Pick up the third ball with your right hand and say, "This one I'll place in my pocket." Place your right hand in your pocket, but finger-palm the ball and bring your hand out again with the ball, and place your hand, palm-down on the table.

Now say, "How many balls are in my left hand?" Someone answers: "Two." Open your left hand and let the three balls drop on the table. "You're not paying attention. I'll do it again. Watch! I'll place one in my left hand." Pick up a ball with your right hand and place it (and the palmed ball) in your left hand. Close your left hand so that the extra ball won't be seen. Pick up another ball and place it in your left fist, through the top (thumb up). "This one I'll place in my pocket." Pick up the third ball and leave it in your pocket.

Now ask, "How many balls in my left hand?" Someone answers: "Two." Open your hand; show that you have three balls.

Say, "Now we'll use just two balls." Place one ball in your pocket. Say, "I'll hold one and I'll place the other one in your hand. When I do, I want you to close your hand very tight—quickly so that nothing can get in or out."

Pick up one of the balls and pretend to place it in your left hand but really keep it in your right one.

Pick up the other ball in your right hand, adding it to the ball you apparently placed in your left hand. Slightly squeeze the balls together so they appear as one and place them in the spectator's hand. Ask him how many he has, and how many you have. He will say you each have one. Open your left hand and show it is empty. While you are placing the balls in the spectator's hand, reach in your pocket with your right hand, get the quarter, finger-palm it, and bring your hand out.

Ask the spectator to open his hand. He has two balls. Take the two from him, and place them on the table. Pick up one ball and place it in your left hand. Pick up the other one and place it, along with the quarter in your left hand. Close your hand and ask, "How many do I have in my hand this time?" At this point, the spectator will say almost anything. Whatever he says, you say, "No, I'm afraid you're wrong. I have twenty-seven!" They won't believe you, of course, so open your hand enough to let one ball drop, say, "One," let the other one drop, "Two," drop the quarter, "and twenty-five, makes, twenty-seven!" Pick up the money and balls and drop them in your pocket.

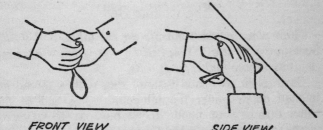

FRONT VIEW   SIDE VIEW

The Bending Spoon

You pick up a spoon from the table and pretend to bend it in half. By waving your hand over it, it is restored.

Pick up the spoon and hold it by its handle. Wave it back and forth a few times. Grip it in your left fist by its handle, handle pointing towards you. Hold it tightly, wrapping your fingers around it as if it were a dagger. Then place the bowl of the spoon down on the table, and wrap your right finger over your left ones. The backs of both hands will be right side up.

Now place your left little finger under the handle, to keep from dropping it, and make a motion as if bending the spoon by pushing down with your hands. Use a lot of false effort, as if it were hard to bend the handle. Hold the spoon still, and move your hands up to a vertical position. You really don't bend the spoon, but this action makes it appear so. Now with your left hand, lift the spoon off the table. It looks as if the bent part of the spoon is in your left fist. The spoon, which sticks out behind your hand, is actually lifted by your little finger which is under the handle. Wave your right hand at the spoon a couple of times, and drop it on the table, showing that it is really not bent at all.

The Rolling Ball

You place a small marble on the table, and it will roll across by itself. You can let your friends examine it, both before and after it rolls.

Before dinner place a small ring with a thread attached to it, under the tablecloth. The end of the thread must run under the tablecloth to a secret assistant across the table. If you don't have time before dinner to have someone help you, you can hold the thread in your lap. But it is more mystifying if the marble rolls away from you.

Place the marble on the hidden ring. Your assistant pulls on the thread and the marble rolls across the table. It should roll slowly. As it is rolling, suggest that someone pick it up and examine it. Then pull the ring away from under the cloth.

If you have time to prepare for the trick before your audience arrives, and do not have an assistant, run the thread across the table over its edge, and back under the table. Then, when you pull on the thread, the ball will roll away from you.

The Traveling Sugar

You place four lumps of sugar on the table, and cover them with your hands. You can make them jump around and finally make all four lumps appear together.

You will need five lumps of sugar, but the audience must be aware of only four. The four lumps are laid on the table so that they form a square. Here is how they look:

3   4

1   2

The extra lump is thumb-palmed (page 64) in your left hand. Now you are ready to start.

Place your right hand over 2, your left hand over 3. With a wiggle of your fingers, your right hand thumb-palms 2, while your left hand leaves the extra lump at 3. Raise your hands slightly, and show that lump number 2 has vanished, and there are two lumps at 3.

Cover 1, with your left hand, and your right hand goes to 3. Wiggle your fingers, lift your hands, palming the lump at 1, in your left hand. Your right hand leaves the lump it has brought over from 2.

Your right hand, which is empty, covers 4, while your left hand covers the three lumps at 3. When you lift your hands, your right hand picks up the lump at 4, and your left hand leaves the fourth lump at 3.

Now the process is reversed. Your left hand covers the four lumps and palms one, while your right hand leaves a lump at 4. Place your left hand over 1, leave a lump there, while your right hand covers, and removes a lump from 3. Place your right hand over 2, leave a lump—and your left hand picks up one of the two lumps at 3.

Now if you lift your left hand an instant before you do your right, the eyes of the audience will go to your right hand, which gives you a chance to drop the extra lump from your left hand into your lap.

The Tumbler Balance

You are able to balance a tumbler or salt shaker, on its edge. Everyone else who tries will fail.

By placing a burnt-out wooden match under the tablecloth, you can lean a tumbler or salt shaker against it, and it will stand at an angle on its edge. If others care to try it, make sure they do so on some other spot on the tablecloth. If they wish to try it where you did it, secretly remove the match.

Rings, Strings, and Pencil

You tie two lengths of string around a pencil, and then around several borrowed rings. Though they are securely knotted, you are able to remove them even while the ends of the string are held.

For this trick, you may borrow everything you need; a pencil, two pieces of string or cord, each about 2 feet long, and as many finger rings as you can. (You must have at least two. You can use napkin rings if no finger rings are available.)

Have someone hold the pencil horizontally, one end

in each hand. Lay the two strings over the pencil with their centers at the top of the pencil and ends hanging down. Using the *two* ends of *one* string as one, and the *two* ends of the *other* as one, tie a simple single knot, pulling it tight against the pencil. Ask the spectator to let go of the pencil, and give him the two strings at one end, and give the other two strings to another spectator. The pencil will hang down from the center between them.

Now take the finger rings and assuming you have borrowed four, hand two to each spectator, and have them thread the two rings over both of the strings they hold. The rings will slide down against the pencil. Ask each spectator to hand you either one of the ends they hold. Take one from each and tie a simple, single knot over the top of the rings. (This knot exchanges the ends and makes the rings look more securely tied.) Tell the spectators to hold their ends tightly. Place your hand over the knots and the rings, and pull out the pencil with the other hand. As soon as the pencil is pulled out, the rings will drop into your hand. Lay the pencil on the table, and open your other hand showing the rings are free. The spectators will now

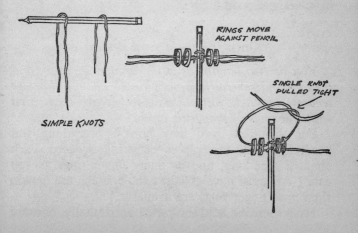

SIMPLE KNOTS

RINGS MOVE AGAINST PENCIL

SINGLE KNOT PULLED TIGHT

hold two strings between them, free of rings and knots.

You can also do this trick in a larger or stage version, by substituting a wand for the pencil, and ropes for the strings. Use large rings to take the place of the finger rings used in this version, or tie several silk handkerchiefs on the ropes. The handkerchiefs will come off the ropes still knotted.

You may recognize the principle used in this trick as the one you used in "Walking Through a Rope" (page 43). In this case, the pencil takes the place of the thread in the other trick.

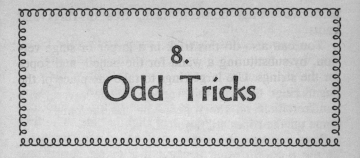

8.
Odd Tricks

In this chapter you will find tricks in which all kinds of objects are used. Most of them can be found around the house. By doing tricks with different things you will add variety and interest to your program.

The Appearing Handkerchief

In this trick, you show that both hands are empty, and when you pull up your sleeves, a handkerchief appears in your hands.

The best kind of handkerchief to use in all magic tricks is silk. Magicians use all sizes. They call them "silks." You will find that a silk about a foot square is the best size to use. A bright color shows up well. You can use a scrap of dress material, or a silk scarf. You should hem the edges so that they won't unravel, unless you buy your silks already hemmed.

To make the handkerchief appear, fold it into a small bundle and place it in the bend of your *left* elbow. Pull a fold of your coat sleeve over it to hide it. Now show that your hands are empty, and pull up your right sleeve. Keep your arms bent all the time, to keep the silk from coming out. Now, pull up your left sleeve and as you do so, get the silk into your right hand and palm it.

Bring your hands together, away from your body, and move them slowly up and down, letting the silk unfold. Now separate your hands, and show the silk. It looks as if it materialized out of thin air.

This trick is best used as the first in a program, because you must keep your arm slightly bent. The first trick in a magician's program is called the "opener." This is a good opener because it is quick, surprising, and attention-getting.

The Vanishing Handkerchief

You pull up your sleeve and roll a silk in your hand. The silk seems to grow smaller and finally vanishes altogether.

Once again, use a 12-inch-square silk. You can use the one you have just produced in the above trick. You also will need a "pull." You can make a pull very easily from a piece of mailing tube about an inch in diameter. Cut a piece of tube about 2 inches long, and paint it black. By means of a piece of wire (paper clip, or hairpin, bent to shape) or a piece of string run through the tube at the end, a piece of elastic cord is attached. The elastic should be about a foot long.

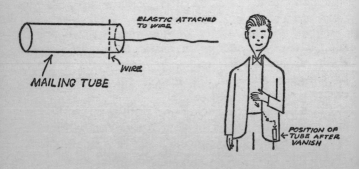

ELASTIC ATTACHED TO WIRE

MAILING TUBE

WIRE

POSITION OF TUBE AFTER VANISH

Tie or pin the free end of elastic to the center of your trousers in the back. You can tie it to your belt-loop; or tie it to a safety pin and then pin it in place. Run the pull through the next belt-loop on your left side. The pull should then hang down on your left hip, but should not show below your coat. Lengthen or shorten the elastic so the pull will be in place.

Now take the pull and place it either in your left trouser pocket, or tuck it in the top of your trousers on the left side so that it may be reached easily.

Hold the silk in your right hand and wave it up and down a couple of times to draw attention to it. Turn slightly so that your left side is away from the audience and get the pull in your left hand. Turn to the front and place your hands together. Move your hands slowly up and down, and stuff the silk slowly into the pull.

When it is all the way in, turn once again to the side so that your left side is away from the audience. Open your hands very slightly, while still moving them up and down as before, so that the pull will fly under your coat out of sight. Face front once again, and continue with the motion of your hands. Slowly, with a wringing motion, open your hands and show that the silk has vanished.

Here and There

This is another method of vanishing or producing a silk. It uses a principle in magic that most people don't realize. That is, you can place a silk in your pocket, and still pull the pocket out to show it is empty.

Put a silk in your pocket and push it up to the top and towards the center of your body. You will find a space large enough to conceal a silk or a small object. If you pull your pocket out, the silk won't show.

So you see, you could produce a silk by the method in "The Appearing Handkerchief" (page 79), and place it in your pocket. After you say a magic word, pull out your pocket and the silk has vanished. Place a silk in your pocket, show that your pocket is empty, then produce the silk from that same pocket by pulling it down with your thumb as you push your pocket back in and vanish it by the method shown in "The Vanishing Handkerchief" (page 80).

The Wandering Silk

You wrap a small silk in several sheets of paper. This is held by a spectator. The silk is removed from the paper bundle, it vanishes, and is found back in the bundle held by the spectator.

You will need two duplicate silks. Place one in the breast pocket of your coat. The other one should be folded into a small bundle and placed in your left coat pocket. You also need a pull (page 80).

Ask a spectator to help you. As he is coming up to the platform, take the silk *secretly* out of your coat pocket and palm it (page 3) in your left hand. Have several sheets of paper napkins lying on your table. Ask the spectator to hand you one sheet. Take it in your right hand, and lay it over your left hand, which contains the palmed-silk. Crush the sheet of paper around the silk and make a small ball.

Ask for another sheet, and take the silk out of your breast pocket, show it and wrap it in the second sheet of paper, crushing it with the first sheet and silk. The audience believes that you have taken a silk out of your pocket and wrapped it in a sheet of paper. Hand the bundle to the spectator and have him go over to the other side of the stage and hold the bundle up so that everyone can see it.

Now announce that you are going to cause the handkerchief to leave the bundle of paper in the spectator's hands, and fly into your hand. Make several motions towards the paper held by the spectator. Act as if the trick has gone wrong because the handkerchief stays in the paper instead of flying into your hand. Go over to the spectator and see if the handkerchief is still there. Open the bundle and remove one of the silks. Be careful not to let the one still in the paper show. Tell your audience that you are going to do the trick backwards, that instead of having the handkerchief come to you, you are going to cause it to go to the spectator. The audience thinks you have removed the only silk from the paper. They don't know that you had placed two silks in the paper at the start of the trick. They believe the paper is now empty.

Now walk back to the other end of the stage, away from the spectator, and as you do so, get the pull in your left hand. Vanish the silk by the pull, and make a waving motion towards the bundle with your hands. Now tell the audience that the handkerchief has returned to the paper held by the spectator. Ask him to open the bundle and he will find the silk inside. It looks as if you had caused it to fly back invisibly to the paper held by the spectator.

The Prayer Bottle

You show a small bottle and a short length of rope. As you tell a story about an old Chinese magician, you place the rope in the neck of the bottle, turn it upside down, and the rope stays in the bottle. You then turn the bottle upright, grasp the rope and the bottle hangs from it. Both bottle and rope may be examined as they are ordinary ones.

You will need a bottle with a narrow neck. It should either be painted or made of very dark glass.

You will also need a piece of stiff clothesline about 10 inches long, and a small rubber or cork ball, small enough to drop easily into the bottle. The diameter of the rope and ball together should be slightly larger then the neck of the bottle.

Start with the ball in the bottle—the ball cannot be seen—and the rope lying nearby. Tell about a Chinese magician who would ask a prayer every day using this bottle. Push the rope into the bottle so that its end touches the bottom.

Turn the bottle upside down by the neck, holding the rope so it won't fall out. The ball will roll down into the neck of the bottle and wedge itself against the rope and sides of the bottle neck. Pull on the rope slightly to make a tight wedge. Let go of the rope and hold the bottle by its bottom, your hand not touching the rope.

Now continue your story and say that if the magician's prayer was to be answered, the rope would stay in the bottle. If it was a very big prayer, he would try something else. Take the rope in your other hand, and let the bottle swing freely on it.

Now place the bottle on the table and push the rope down into the bottle. This causes the ball to drop down into the bottle. You can now remove the rope. Just lift it right out and drop it on the table, or hand it to a spectator to examine. Pick up the bottle by its neck and turn it upside down. The ball will roll into your hand. Hold it in the thumb-palm position (page 64) and say, "You see there are no hooks on the bottom." Turn the bottle right side up and place it on the table. Let the spectators examine it, as well as the rope. While they are doing this, slip the ball into your pocket.

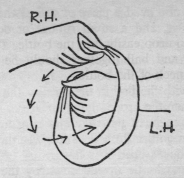

The Dissolving Knot

Tie what appears to be a tight knot in a silk. When the ends are pulled, the knot dissolves.

Hold the silk in your hands by diagonally opposite corners. Bring your right hand away from your body, and place the end of the silk over your left wrist. This will form a loop. Thrust the right-hand-end through this loop from the side away from your body. Now when the ends are pulled, the knot will dissolve.

This trick is not always easy to learn. You have to get the "feel" of it. The only way is to try and keep trying, following the directions very carefully, until you get it.

After you push the right end through the loop, the silk will be wrapped around your wrists. Hold the ends tightly, and let the center part of the silk fall off your wrists, while you pull on the ends. Once you have learned how to do this, you should do it quite rapidly.

Knot Here!

You hold a handkerchief by its corner and let it hang down. When you shake it, a knot appears tied in its corner.

Tie a knot in the corner of a silk handkerchief. Hold the knot between the thumb and forefinger of your right hand.

Show the silk, and take the corner that is hanging down, between the thumb and forefinger of your left hand. Shake the silk several times and on the final shake (a hard snap), open the fingers of your right hand and let go of the silk. The knot appears on the silk held in your left hand. This gives the illusion that the knot shakes itself into the corner of the handkerchief.

The Escaping Matchbox

You hang an empty matchbox on a ribbon or string by pushing the ribbon between the drawer and the cover. You are able to remove the box while the ends of the ribbon are held by spectators.

Pull or cut one side of a matchbox cover so that one side and the top lift up like a hinge. Put a daub of beeswax or "magicians' wax" on the inside and press it back so the cover will look whole.

Open the box and push the ribbon through from end to end and close the box. Cover it with a handkerchief, and have a spectator hold the ends of the ribbon. Reach under the handkerchief, lift up the side of the box, and slip it off the ribbon. Press the sides of the cover back in place so that it stays together. Remove the box from under the handkerchief, and then lift the handkerchief from the ribbon, while the spectator still holds the ends of the ribbon.

Find the Rattle

You place a penny in an empty matchbox and mix it up with two other boxes which are empty. No one is able to find the box that contains the penny, even though it rattles.

Get four small matchboxes. Put a penny in one, close it and fasten it to your left wrist with a wide rubber band, or ribbon. It should be under your coat sleeve, hidden from view.

Place the three empty boxes on the table and borrow a penny. Drop it into one of the boxes, and as you close the box, let the penny slip out of the box into your hand. Hold it in the finger-palm position (page 3). Close the other two boxes, and move them around on the table so that no one can tell which is which. Pick up one of the boxes in your left hand, and shake it. It will sound as if it has a penny inside, because of the box in your sleeve. Tell the audience they must keep their eyes on the box that rattles. Then ask them to point to a box, to see if it is the one that rattles. Either pick up with your right hand the one that they point to, or let them pick it up and shake it. It will be empty.

Now pick up one of the other boxes, and shake it with your left hand so that it rattles. Tell them to follow the box closely. Repeat this several times. They are never able to find the box that rattles.

At the end of the trick, have someone pick up the box. This one won't rattle. Ask someone else to pick a box that rattles from the remaining two. But this one doesn't rattle either. Now pick up the last box with your right hand, and open it. As you pick it up, let the penny that you have palmed drop on the table, as if it had come from the box.

Eggs-Actly

Here are a couple of little stunts that have to do with eggs.

The first deals with the art of spinning an egg. No

one is able to spin an egg but you. It's very easy. Just use fresh raw eggs for the spectators to spin, and a hard-boiled one for yourself. The fresh ones won't spin, but the hard-boiled one will.

Hand someone an egg. Ask him to balance it on its end. He'll say it can't be done. You can do this either by shaking the egg so that the yolk settles, or by putting a small amount of salt on the tablecloth, and making a little mound. Press the egg carefully into the salt, and it will balance.

The Climbing Ring

You drop a borrowed ring over the end of a pencil. You make it climb up and down the pencil, and start and stop on command. At the end of the trick, the spectators examine the ring and the pencil.

Use a pencil with an eraser. Push a straight pin into the eraser, so that it doesn't show. Tie a length of black thread to the pin, and tie the other end of the thread to your vest or suit button. If you wish, you may eliminate the pin, and just tie the thread to the top of the pencil, and the other end to your button. Place the pencil in your outside breast pocket.

Borrow a finger ring, and hold the pencil with the eraser pointing up. Drop the ring over the end of the pencil and thread. Be sure to have enough slack in the thread so that the ring will drop to the bottom end of the pencil.

Now, by moving the pencil slowly away from your body, you make the ring climb up the pencil. Command the ring to stop, and simply hold your hand still. To make the ring go down the pencil, slowly move your hand closer to your body.

Turn the pencil upside down, and let the ring drop off, into your hand. Hand it back to the spectator. As you do this, either pull the pin out of the eraser, or slip it off the top of the pencil if it is tied, and hand the pencil around for examination.

Shirt-Off

You walk up to a spectator, unbutton the cuffs of his shirt, and remove his tie. You then reach behind his neck, grab the collar of his shirt and pull it up and off over his head. His coat will remain buttoned as before.

Once again you will need a secret assistant. Before you begin your show, have him come to you to prepare secretly. He must first remove his coat, shirt and tie. Drape his shirt over his back, like a cape. Do not put his arms through the sleeves of his shirt. Bring his collar around to the front and button the first two shirt buttons. Put his tie on and tie it in the regular way. Button the cuffs of his shirt around his wrists so that his sleeves lie along his arms. Now have him put on his coat, and sit in the audience.

When you are ready to do the shirt trick, ask for a spectator to help you. Have your secret assistant volunteer to come up. Admire his tie, and remove it. Unbutton the top two buttons of his shirt. Now unbutton his shirt cuffs. Reach behind his neck, grasp the back of his shirt collar, and with a sudden sweep of your arm pull his shirt completely off, over his head. He will stand there in his coat, with his shirt gone. This is a very funny stunt.

Egg From Nowhere

You show a pocket handkerchief, fold it up and produce several eggs which you drop into a borrowed hat. The hat when returned to the owner is empty.

You may use a fake wooden egg, or a rubber ball for this trick. Push a thumbtack into the end of the egg. You will also need a man's large handkerchief. Attach a short length of black thread to the egg or ball by tying it around the thumbtack. The other end of the thread is attached to the center of one edge of the handkerchief, so that if the handkerchief were held up by the two corners of that edge, the egg would hang in the center of the handkerchief. Lay the handkerchief on the table, in such way that you can pick it up by the corners causing the egg to hang out of sight.

Borrow a man's hat and place it on the table. Pick

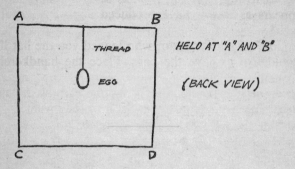

THREAD

EGG

HELD AT "A" AND "B"

(BACK VIEW)

up the handkerchief so that the egg hangs behind it and is not seen by your audience. Bring the two top corners together and hold them between the thumb and forefinger of your right hand. Grasp the two cor-

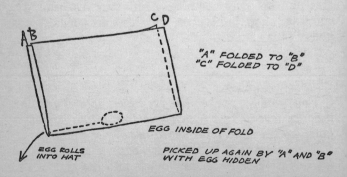

"A" FOLDED TO "B"
"C" FOLDED TO "D"

EGG INSIDE OF FOLD

EGG ROLLS
INTO HAT

PICKED UP AGAIN BY "A" AND "B"
WITH EGG HIDDEN

ners that are hanging down with your left hand. Now bring your right and left hands to a horizontal position. Tip one end of the handkerchief, so that the egg will roll along the inside center of it and fall out the other end into the hat. Drop the handkerchief on the edge of the hat, reach in and show the egg by lifting it from the hat. Drop it back into the hat, and pick up the handkerchief by the four corners, two in each hand. Produce another egg in the same way, by letting it roll into the hat. Make sure the audience can see the egg as it drops in. Repeat this several times, until it appears as if you have produced almost a hatful of eggs.

Now ask the spectator who loaned you the hat if he would like to have the eggs. Place the handkerchief (with the egg wrapped inside) in your pocket. Pick up the hat and pretend to throw the eggs at the audience. The hat is empty. Return it to the owner.

9.
Advanced Tricks

By now you may feel ready to advance to some of the more difficult tricks. These tricks have been selected because they are easy to do, but look professional. In fact, they are!

The Sympathetic Silks

You show six silks, each about 18 inches square. They may be all one color, or three of one color, red, and three of another, green. You tie the three red silks together, and hang them over the back of a chair. The green ones are hung over the back of another chair. You say the magic words, and the knots change places. The red ones are now separate, and the green ones tied together.

Before you start, tie the corners of the green silks together with a tight knot. To make them appear as single silks, hold them up by the corners next to (not opposite from) the knots. The knots will be hidden in the folds of the silks.

You must learn how to tie the red silks together with a "dissolving knot," so that they will look as if they are tied tightly, but will come apart when you wish. To do this, begin as if you were going to tie the silks in a genuine knot. The first part of the knot which you make quickly, is nothing but a twist. The second part, which seems to make the knot complete, is a simple single knot. The motion of the tying, and the appearance of the knot when tied, give it a genuine look.

To start the trick, either hold the silks in your hands, by the top corners, or have them lying on a chair. Show them to your audience, and count them from hand to hand. You can do this, if you keep your hands together, even though three of them are tied. Lay the three green (knotted) silks over the back of a chair. Tie the red ones together using the special knot, and place them over the back of another chair. Call attention to the fact that the red ones are tied. Command the knots to change places. Then pretend you are carrying the invisible knots from one chair to another.

Pick up the green silk on the end of the chain of three by the corner diagonally opposite the hidden knots, and show that they are tied. Then pick up a corner of the red silk but pick it up suddenly and give it a slight snap. The red handkerchiefs will be unknotted and separate.

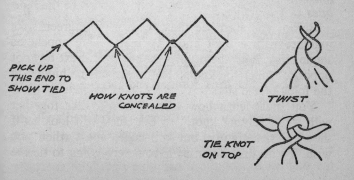

PICK UP
THIS END TO
SHOW TIED

HOW KNOTS ARE
CONCEALED

TWIST

TIE KNOT
ON TOP

Crazy Silks

Two handkerchiefs change color, change places, and multiply.

You will need four silks, two red and two blue, about 12 inches square. You will also need a bag and a candy "kiss." Make the bag about 7 inches square, with a cloth partition running the length of the bag, dividing it into two sections or compartments.

Before you start, place one of the blue silks in your right trouser pocket, and one red one in your left pocket. Push them both up to the corners so the pockets may be shown empty, as explained in "Here and There."

In one side of the bag place the other red silk and put the blue one on top of it. Place the candy kiss in your right outside coat pocket.

Get a lady or girl to help you with the trick and have her stand next to you, facing the audience. Show that the bag is empty by turning it inside out. Say you found it and it must belong to someone very poor because it is empty. Show that your pockets are empty, and say that you are very poor, too. As you push your pockets back in, push the handkerchiefs down into the pocket proper. Reach in the bag and act very suprised and pull out the blue silk. Hand it to the lady and ask her to put it back in the bag. Have her put it on the empty side, then open the other side. Ask her to take it out again and this time she gets the red one. All through this trick you must act surprised. This is what makes the trick funnier and more enjoyable to the audience.

Reach into your right trouser pocket and pull out the blue silk. Act as if it had disappeared fom the bag and jumped into your pocket. Put the blue silk into the bag on top of the other blue one. The spectator still holds the red one. Reach in your left pocket and bring out the other red one. Place both red ones into the empty side of the bag. Have the lady reach into the bag and take out the blue ones. Show that the two red ones have changed to blue. Put them back in the bag on top of the red ones. Now show that the bag is empty, by turning it inside out. Hold the bag in your left hand. Put it close to the lady's eyes and ask her to look into the bag. While she is looking into it reach in your right coat pocket and get the candy kiss. Bring the bag back in front of you, and put your right hand into the bag, leaving the candy inside. Say, "Yes, it is really empty, but if you reach in the bag again you'll get a kiss!" Have her pull out the candy kiss. Thank her for helping you, and let her keep the kiss.

The 20th Century Silks

You tie two handkerchiefs together and place them in full sight. A third handkerchief is shown which vanishes. It is finally found tied securely between the first two handkerchiefs.

You will need one red or light-colored silk, one dark blue silk, two variegated or "rainbow" silks which match, and a pull (page 80). The colors in the

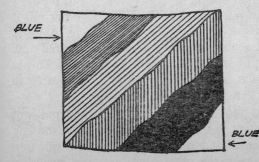

BLUE

BLUE

RAINBOW SILK

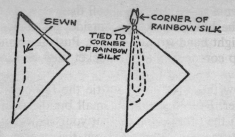

rainbow silks should run diagonally, and two of the corners in each silk should be blue to match the blue silk.

Fold the blue silk diagonally in half, and sew a "pocket" in a curved line almost the length of the silk from top to bottom. Tie one of the rainbow silks to the corner of the blue silk, and tuck it down inside of the blue one, center first. The other end of the rainbow is left exposed so that it looks like the corner of the blue silk. Place the pull where you can reach it easily.

Hold the three silks up by the top corners, and tie the red and blue silks together. You actually tie the red to the corner of the concealed rainbow. Place the two tied silks behind your neck, or over the back of a chair with the knots to the rear. Or, roll them up, and tuck them, knotted end first, into a glass. Vanish the duplicate rainbow silk with the pull. Grasp the end of the red silk and give it a sharp pull. The rainbow will be pulled out of the blue silk, and the three silks will appear knotted.

Another 20th Century

Here is another way of creating the same effect without using prepared or sewn silks.

You will need six silks, two red, two blue, and two yellow, all about 12 inches square. Tie a yellow silk between a red and a blue. Roll these in a small bundle with the blue one on the outside, and place them in your right hand trouser pocket. Push the bundle up to the top corner so that the pocket may be shown to be empty.

Show the three silks and tie the red and blue ones together. Roll them into a small bundle with the blue one on the outside. Show that your right hand trouser pocket is empty by pulling out the pocket. Place the silks in your pocket. Tell your audience that the corner of the handkerchiefs will be in view at all times. Pull the corner of the blue silks (the one that has the red and yellow tied to it) out of your pocket. Vanish the yellow silk by placing it in your left trouser pocket (page 80). Command the yellow handkerchief to join the red and the blue. Grasp the corner of the blue silk that is in sight, and pull it. The silks will unroll, showing the yellow one tied between the other two. Now, casually show that your right pocket is empty, pushing up the remaining silks so that they do not show. You have already shown that your left pocket is empty, when the silk vanished from there.

You can also use the special bag (page 94) instead of your pockets to perform this trick.

The Miser's Dream

You will surprise and please your audience by producing a seemingly endless number of coins from the air. You drop them into a bucket to make them rattle and clink.

You will need a small children's sand-bucket, or a plastic or metal cup that is opaque, and several real or palming coins.

Place about four or five coins in a neat stack on your table *behind* the bucket. Place four coins in your left coat pocket, and one coin in your right coat pocket.

It is also necessary to learn one simple sleight-of-hand move with a coin. The coin should be held edgewise or flat in the crotch of your right thumb and first finger. If it is held properly you will find that you can open and close your first finger and the coin will stay in place. Now, if you bend your fingers as if to close the hand, the coin may be grasped flatwise between your first and second fingers. Straighten your fingers, and the coin will be displayed. By closing your fingers again, the coin will once again be hidden in the crotch of the thumb. Practice moving the coin from the tips of your fingers back to the crotch of your thumb until you can do it quickly and smoothly. If a throwing motion is used when the coin is made to vanish (into the crotch of the thumb) the coin will not be seen.

To begin the routine, obtain the coin from your right pocket and hold it in the thumb crotch position as explained above. Pick up the bucket in your right hand and show it to be ordinary and empty. As you show the bucket, your left hand secretly picks up the stack of coins from the table. Hold these in the finger-palm position (page 3). Take the bucket in your left hand, from your right hand, and hold it so that your left fingers are inside the bucket, with the coins against the inside of the bucket. Your left thumb will be outside the bucket.

Thrust your right hand into the air, and apparently "catch" a coin between your fingers. What you do is to bend your fingers in and grasp the coin bringing it into view. Put your right hand into the bucket, and get the coin back into the thumb crotch position, and at the same time, let one of the coins held in your left hand drop into the bucket. The audience will hear the coin fall into the bucket, and think that it is the coin that you had in your right hand. Take your right hand out of the bucket, and it will appear empty. Once again reach into the air and catch "another" coin, and drop it into the bucket. Of course you really drop one from your left hand.

After all the coins are produced, that is, all the coins you held in your left hand, have been dropped into the bucket, you will still have one coin in your right hand. Produce this in your right hand and drop it into the bucket. Always keep the bucket moving so that the coins inside the bucket will rattle and make a lot of noise. Now your right hand will be empty, while your left hand still holds the bucket.

Reach into the bucket with your right hand and remove the coins. Place the bucket on the table, and drop the coins from your right hand one at a time into it. As you do this, remove the coins from your left coat pocket, finger-palm them, and pick up the bucket again with your left hand so that the coins go inside it once again as before. Reach into the bucket with your right hand and stir the coins around. Get one of the coins in the thumb crotch position, and take out your hand which will appear empty.

Produce a coin from behind your neck, show it, and instead of putting your hand inside the bucket, make a throwing motion toward the bucket. Pretend to see the coin go through the air, and follow it with your eyes, and as the coin seems to arrive at the bucket, drop one in from your left hand, so that it is heard to fall. Now begin producing coins from behind your knee, from a lady's hair, or anywhere you wish. Don't always drop a coin from your left hand as you apparently place the coin in the bucket, merely shake the bucket and make a noise. Or you can make a noise by hitting the top edge of the bucket with your right hand.

Produce the rest of the coins, by allowing them to drop from your left hand. Produce the last coin from your right hand and actually throw it into the air so that it lands in the bucket. Then take a bow.

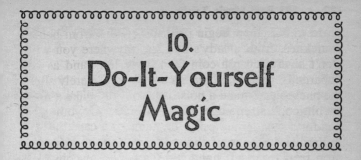

10.
Do-It-Yourself Magic

Many of you will find that you not only enjoy doing tricks, but have other interests as well, such as building things in your home shop. The tricks in this chapter are easy to make yourself. You will probably have as much fun making the apparatus as you will in performing the tricks themselves. Some of these tricks don't even require tools, and none require elaborate building.

Message From the Dead

A slate is first carefully cleaned on both sides, wrapped in a sheet of newspaper, and when unwrapped you find the magical appearance of a "message from the dead."

In a dime store buy a school slate about 7 by 9 inches with a narrow wooden frame around it. Take a piece of cardboard and cut it to fit the slate inside the frame. Paint one side of the cardboard with dead black, or blackboard paint and on its other side paste a sheet of newspaper. The "flap," as magicians call it, should fit snugly enough inside the frame so that it will not move about when you clean the slate, and loosely enough so that it will drop out when the slate is turned upside down.

On one side of the slate print a message like "Merry Christmas," "Happy Easter," or "Greetings!" Place the flap over the message, with the black side of the flap out, so the slate looks ordinary. Or, instead of a message you could print the name of a card that you intend to force (page 4) and then reveal it on the slate after the card is selected (a two-in-one trick).

Show the slate, holding it by its edges, your thumb on one side and fingers on the other to hold the flap in place. Clean the slate on both sides. Wrap it in a sheet of newspaper, flap side down, and lay it on the table. Now call on the "spirits" to write a message. Unwrap the slate, leaving the flap on the newspaper. The flap will not show on the newspaper, because of the paper pasted on its back. Hold the slate up and reveal the message the spirits have written.

The Rising Cards

Three cards are selected by members of the audience and replaced in the deck. The deck is shuffled by a spectator, and you place it in a glass goblet. The cards rise one at a time from the goblet!

For this trick you will need a deck of cards, ten or more extra cards, a glass goblet large enough to hold the deck, and a length of black thread.

The goblet is unprepared and so is the deck. Take one of the extra cards (they must be from another deck, as their duplicates must be in the regular deck you use) and make a slit at the top center of the card about half an inch long. Slip one end of a length of strong black thread through the slit. Tie a knot in the thread at the front of the card, and pull it tight against the card. Put another card in front of the threaded one so that the thread will not show from the front.

Take another extra card, a duplicate of one that you are going to force, and put it behind this threaded card, so that the thread runs under the force card.

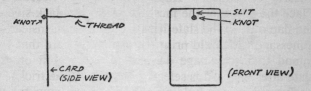

KNOT→ ←THREAD

←CARD
(SIDE VIEW)

SLIT
KNOT

(FRONT VIEW)

Place still another extra card behind this and bring the thread up and over the top of this card. Place the next force card on top of the thread so that the thread runs under it. Place still one more card with the thread over its top, and then the last force card with the thread under it.

Place the rest of the extra cards behind this with the thread over their tops. Now you can see that if the thread is pulled gently, the force cards will rise one at a time from the packet. The free end of the thread is attached to a small nail driven in the back of your table, or tied to a book or other heavy object. Now, if the packet is placed in the goblet, and the goblet pulled forward, the thread will become tight and the cards will rise. Place the packet of cards face-down on the table next to the goblet.

You already know how to force cards (page 4). This is how you use the first force taught you—the one in which the spectator cuts the cards. To force all three cards, place two of the force cards on the bottom of the deck, and the third one on the top. (These cards must match the cards in the special packet you have prepared.) Have a spectator make the cut as in the force. Have him look at the bottom card of the top packet (the card that you would normally have him look at when forcing only one card). After he has looked at the force card, have him remove it from the

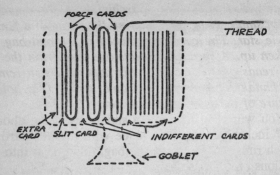

deck, and show the person next to him the next card from the bottom. Now go to another person and have him look at the *top* card of the LOWER portion—the portion that the first spectator held. (This will be the third force card that you placed on the top of the deck at the beginning.)

Now that the three cards have been forced, ask the spectators to remember their cards, and have them replace them in the deck. Give the deck to someone to shuffle. Take the deck and go to your table. Lay the deck face-down on the table, right on top of the prepared packet. As you do this, lift up the goblet in your other hand, and show that it is quite unprepared. Place the goblet on the table towards the rear, and put the deck, along with the prepared packet, into the goblet, card faces towards the audience.

Pick up the goblet, and move it slowly towards the audience. As the thread tightens, the first card will rise from the deck. After it has risen, remove it and show it to the audience, and ask if it was one of the selected cards. Repeat this with the other two cards.

The Magic Frame

You show a small picture frame which contains no picture, only a black background. You cover the frame with a pocket handkerchief, then show about a dozen small cards, each bearing the name of a famous movie star. The cards are placed in a small bag and shaken up. A spectator selects one card from the bag and reads off the name of his selection. You remove the handkerchief from the frame, and it now holds a picture of the selected movie star.

You will need to make a small cloth bag, about 6 or 7 inches square. It is made with a cloth partition which runs the length of the bag, dividing it into two sections or compartments.

You will also need an easel picture frame with a piece of black cloth glued to the inside of the back, so that the frame has a black background when empty. Cut a piece of black cloth, the same width as the inner edge of the frame but about three inches longer, out of the same material as the background.

Now, cut a picture of a famous movie star out of a magazine, so that it will fit in the frame. Take twenty-four pieces of cardboard and print the name of this movie star on thirteen of them. On the remaining eleven cards print the names of eleven different movie stars.

Before you start the trick, place the eleven different name cards, plus one of the thirteen duplicate cards, in one side of the bag. Place the twelve duplicates in the other compartment.

Arrange the frame like this, starting from the front: first the glass, then the piece of black cloth, then the picture, and finally the background. The cloth will stick out of the top of the frame, and hang down the back.

To begin, reach into the bag and pull out the cards that bear the different names. Have a spectator look at them. While he is doing this, show the audience that the frame is empty. Place it standing up, on your table, and cover it with a thick pocket handkerchief.

Have the person who looked at the cards drop them into the bag. (Make sure they go into the empty side.) Shake the bag to mix the cards, then hold the bag open and ask the spectator to reach into it and remove one of the cards. Make sure to hold open the side with the duplicate cards. Ask him to read the name aloud on the card he has selected.

Pull the handkerchief off the frame, and as you do so, pull the black cloth out and off, hiding it in the folds of the handkerchief. You can feel the cloth through the handkerchief. Hold up the frame and show the picture. If you wish, you may take the frame apart and show that it is ordinary.

You don't have to use movie stars, for this trick. You might want to use presidents, or other historical persons. Instead of using a picture, you could force a card (page 4) and have a duplicate in the frame. You then would not need the bag. A bag is quite useful, however, as it can be used in other tricks. (See page 94.)

The Wand and Ball

You show a magic wand and a Ping-Pong ball. The wand is held horizontally in one hand and the ball is placed on the center of the wand by your other hand. The ball balances on the wand and rolls along its edge.

First you must make a wand. Use a piece of wood dowel 12 inches long and ½ inch in diameter. Paint the wand black except for about 1 inch at each end. Paint these "tips" white to make the wand easier for the audience to see.

You will also use a Ping-Pong ball which is not prepared, and two straight pins or small brads, and a piece of strong black thread. Stick one of the pins into the wand about 1 inch from the end. Push the other pin about 1 inch from the other end of the wand. Now tie one end of the thread to one of the pins, and stretch it out taut and tie it to the other pin. Now if you hold up the wand, the thread won't show because the wand and thread are both black. Be sure not to push the pins into the wand too far, as the thread and the edge of the wand form a "track" for the ball to balance on.

Show the wand to the audience by waving it. Pick up the ball and bounce it so that the audience can see that it is unprepared. Hold the wand horizontally in one hand by its end with the pins and thread toward you. Carefully place the ball on the thread and wand so that it will balance. Sometimes it is best to rotate the wand so that the thread is slightly higher than the edge of the wand. This makes the balancing easier. If the ball won't stay balanced, you have pushed the pins in too far. It is best to let the ball fall a few times so that it will look as if the trick is a real feat of juggling. If you make it look too easy, people will think you have something attached to the ball.

After you have balanced the ball on the wand, hold the wand in both hands and tilt the wand slightly and allow the ball to roll back and forth along it. Reach up and take the ball off the wand and toss it to someone in the audience. Either place the wand on the table, or secretly pull out the pins and pass the wand around for examination.

Dyeing the Silks

A sheet of paper is formed into a tube, and a white silk is pushed through it. When it comes out the other end of the tube, it has changed color. This is repeated with two other white silks, and the tube is shown to be empty at the finish.

You will need three white silks, and three colored

silks, all about 12 by 12 inches. Cut a piece of heavy "construction" paper to about 8 by 11 inches. Make a small screen out of cardboard. It should fold lengthwise down the center and should be about 14 inches across, before folding, and about 10 inches high. Decorate it any way you wish and make it heavy enough to stand up by itself. You will use this to display the silks, and also to hide the dye-tube.

The dye-tube is made from a piece of mailing tube 1½ inches in diameter, and 4 inches long. It is never seen by the audience. A cloth tape is attached in the inside center of the tube by its ends so that the center fold of the tape will come flush to either end of the

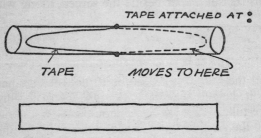

TAPE ATTACHED AT ●

TAPE   MOVES TO HERE

TAPE ABOUT SAME LENGTH AS TUBE

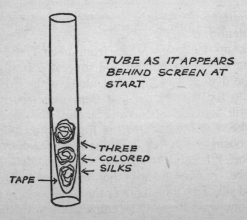

TUBE AS IT APPEARS
BEHIND SCREEN AT
START

THREE
COLORED
SILKS

TAPE

tube. You will also need a piece of sticky tape to hold
the paper tube closed.

In one end of the dye-tube place the three colored
silks, one at a time, and push them down into the tube
as far as they will go. They will go on top of the tape
and clear to the other end of the tube, but they won't
fall out, because the cloth tape will stop them. Now,
stand the screen up on your table, the fold towards the
audience, and behind it stand the dye-tube. The end
which has the tape showing and holds the silks in the
tube should be next to the table. Drape the three white
silks over the top of the screen so that they hang down
in front more than they do at the back. Lay the sheet
of construction paper beside the screen, along with the
sticky tape.

To start the trick, pick up the construction paper
and form it into a long tube, just a little larger in diameter than the dye-tube. Place the piece of sticky tape
around the middle of the tube to hold it together and
stand it behind the screen, right over the top of
the dye-tube. The paper tube should stick out above the
top of the screen. As you place the tube behind the
screen, you should pick up one of the white silks from
the screen, with your other hand to divert the audience's attention. Display the silk to the audience and
call attention to its color.

Pick up the paper tube from behind the screen,
holding it near its bottom and squeezing it slightly so
that the dye-tube comes right along with it. Push the
silk into the paper tube and thus, into the dye-tube.
You will be pushing the silk against the tape in the
dye-tube, which will force the first colored silk out of
the opposite end of the dye-tube and then into the paper tube. When the white silk is completely hidden in
the tube, reach in the other end and remove the
colored silk. Lay this silk over the screen where the first
white one was. Repeat the same thing with the other

two white silks, placing the colored ones on the screen. After you have "dyed" all three white silks, and placed them on the screen, hold the paper tube in one hand, and pick up the three colored silks in your other. As you are reaching over for the silks, the hand holding the tube should bring the lower end of the tube behind the screen for an instant. As you do this, release the pressure on the paper tube and let the dye-tube fall out behind the screen. It is best to have a box or container with a soft pad in its bottom behind the screen so that the dye-tube will not make a noise or roll off the table when it is dropped behind the screen.

Place the silks back on the screen and either tear up or unroll the paper tube to show it is empty. You should say something about the colors of the silks as you pick them up this last time, so as not to arouse suspicion.

Silk From Paper

You show a small square of paper. It is formed into a cone and a handkerchief is produced from it.

For this trick you will need to make a "gimmick" which is the magicians' word for a small piece of secret apparatus used to perform a trick, such as a pull. The gimmick is made of stiff paper, and is just large enough to hold a small silk. It will measure about 2½ inches long, and is made in the shape of a small cone. It will be about 1½ inches across the mouth of the cone. The closed end of the cone should be snipped off so that the opening will be large enough for you to place your second finger inside the cone.

Place a small silk in this gimmick and lay it on the table with the small hole towards you. Lay a sheet of heavy opaque paper, about 8 by 10 inches, over the gimmick to hide it.

Pick up the paper by one end in your right hand, slipping your fingers underneath it. Get your second finger in the cone and pick it up with the paper but keep it behind the paper. Now, as you bring up the paper, grasp it in your left hand, with your fingers in front. Your right thumb will be in the front of the paper. Bring your right forefinger to the front; swing your hand over, so that all your fingers, except your second one go to the front. Your thumb will now go to the back of the paper.

Slide your hands around the paper, so as to hold the paper, near the top, by the long edges. Handle the paper very casually. Grasp the bottom of the paper with your left hand and bring it up around the back of your hand, forming a cone, enclosing the gimmick. Remove your right finger from the cone, and hold the cone at the bottom to keep it from unrolling. Reach in the cone with your left hand and produce the silk. You may either remove the gimmick with your right finger, hiding it under the silk and showing the empty cone, or ball up the cone (and gimmick) and toss it aside.

The Famous Chinese Laundry Ticket

You show a strip of paper with some Chinese characters on it. It is torn up and folded and when the pieces are unfolded, the strip is restored, though a small bundle of paper falls to the floor. The audience believes these to be the torn pieces, but when the bundle is opened, they receive a surprise.

Cut two strips of paper 10 inches long and 3 inches wide. Letter the two strips with Chinese characters. Just make some characters that look oriental if you don't know where to find some real Chinese characters to copy. The characters on the two strips should match exactly.

Yellow is a good color for the papers as it shows up well and looks oriental. Use black ink to print the letters. You will also need one strip of paper the same size as the two duplicates, with the words: "So Sorry, Please," printed on it. You will also need some paste, or rubber cement.

Lay the two duplicate papers back to back, with the writing on the outside, and paste them together at one small spot only. Make the spot of paste about an inch square, and about 3 inches from the top of the strips, right behind one of the characters.

Now, very carefully, fold one of the papers down from the top at the edge of the pasted area, and crease it. Fold it from the bottom up to the pasted area. Continue folding until you have the paper folded into a small bundle about the width of the pasted part. Then

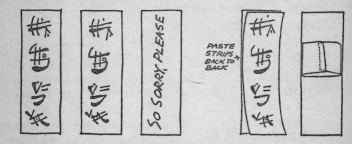

fold in the sides of the strip and tuck one end in the other so it won't unfold. If you now pick up the unfolded paper, you will find that the folded one will be behind it and will not show from the front. Roll the unfolded paper around the folded one.

Take the other paper with the "So Sorry, Please" written on it, and fold it into a small packet about the same size as the paper on the back of the Chinese paper. Place this paper under your right armpit, before you start the trick, so it will fall to the floor when you want it to.

To start the trick, unroll the ticket and display it to the audience. Hold it in your right hand at the top (near the folded piece), and your left hand at the bottom, and straighten it out somewhat by stretching it between your hands. Tear the top portion crosswise below the folded paper. Place this piece behind the longer strips, and tear it once again, so you will have three pieces about the same size. Now, in your hands, you will hold from back to front: the folded piece, and the torn piece to which it is attached, and the other two torn pieces.

Begin to fold the torn pieces into a bundle the same size as the folded piece. Fold it good and tight, and place this bundle in your left hand and squeeze the pieces together. Turn over the bundle and be careful not to expose the torn pieces at the back of the whole piece as you unfold the whole piece. Unfold it completely, and show the spectators that it has been restored.

As you do so, raise your right arm slightly and let the third piece fall to the floor. Try to look very embarrassed, and then try to hide it by putting your foot over it. Put the piece you have just "restored" on your table, and be sure the pieces don't show. Now act as if you were "caught." The audience will tell you about the piece on the floor. Pick up the piece on the floor, and begin to unfold it as if you were very unhappy. When you unfold the paper, smile and let the audience have time to read the message. Now they see that the joke was on them!

Make up several sets of papers at one time, so that if you have to do a trick at a moment's notice you will be prepared. Of course, you can use the "So Sorry" paper over and over again.

The Block Through the Hat

You borrow a hat from a spectator, and show a small block of wood and a small cardboard container just large enough to hold the wooden block. The block is placed in the container and can be seen through the large holes in the container. Both are placed on top of the hat. The block vanishes from the container, and is found under the hat.

You will need a block or cube of wood about 2½ inches square. You may decorate this any way you like. You can use letters or numbers, like those on children's blocks, or spots, to represent a die.

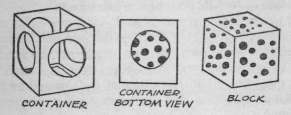

CONTAINER

CONTAINER, BOTTOM VIEW

BLOCK

Make a container out of cardboard just enough larger than the block so the block will slip in and out easily. The container is made with no top, and the sides have large circles cut in them, so the block will show clearly. It actually looks like a sort of frame. The bottom also has a hole like those on the sides, but inside the container you must paste a piece of paper to look like the block. Thus, if you painted the block red, the paper in the bottom of the container would also be red.

You will also need a sheet of newspaper, and a hat which you will borrow from someone in the audience. Place the block inside the container and place it on the table, with the bottom down.

To start the trick, pick up the container and the block. By squeezing the container to keep the block from falling out, show all sides of it, including the bottom. Now turn the container upside down and allow the block to fall into your hand. Keep your hand over the bottom of the container so that the open side will not show. Place the block back into the container.

Wrap the sheet of newspaper around the two, forming a tube with open ends. Turn over the tube so that the open top of the container is down, but hold the block in the container with the pressure of your thumb and fingers on the outside of the paper. Pick up the hat with your other hand, and swing it from left to right as you show it is empty. The hat will naturally swing under the tube, and when it does, relax the pressure on the container, so that the block, and not the container, falls into the hat unnoticed.

The hat, with the block inside it, is placed mouth down on your table. Now dip the end of the tube slightly so that the audience gets a glimpse of the fake end of the container, and they will think the block is still there. Place the tube on top of the hat, and let the container slide down the tube so that it rests on top of the hat. (Be sure the container lands with the open side up.) Unwrap the container and show that it is empty. Now, very slowly lift the hat and reveal the block. The audience can see that the container is empty, but you must lift the hat slowly so that they don't think you slipped the block under the hat. Pick up the block, drop it into the container, and return the hat to its owner.

The Afghan Bands

You show a band of cloth which is in the form of a circle, and tear it into several bands while telling a story about a circus. You will make two bands first, then one large band, and finally two bands, one linked within the other.

Place a strip of plain cotton or muslin cloth (6 inches wide and 24 inches long) on a flat surface. Make three slits 2½ inches long: one of them 1 inch from one edge, one at the center of the band, and the third 1 inch from the other edge. Make these slits at each end of your strip, lengthwise.

Now form the strip into a circle, pasting the ends of the cloth together. Make a half-twist of strip "a" before pasting it permanently. With strip "d" make a full twist before pasting it. The two center parts are pasted without any twists. The cloth when torn down the center and all the way around will form two circles. The circle with the half-twist will form one long continuous circle, while the other one, with the full twist, will form two circles, one linked within the other.

Your story goes like this: "The other day I went to the circus. First of all I went to the Side Show, and found the manager very upset. I asked him what the trouble was and he said, 'I have no belt for the Fat-Lady, or for the Siamese Twins.' I asked him if he had a belt that no one was using. He said he had only this wide belt (Show the strip) which belonged to the Strong-Man. I told him I was a magician, and asked to borrow the belt. I tore the belt in two like this! (Tear the strip in two so that you have two strips.) 'Now,' I said, 'we have two belts.' 'Yes,' he said, 'but

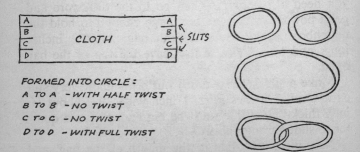

FORMED INTO CIRCLE :

A TO A – WITH HALF TWIST

B TO B – NO TWIST

C TO C – NO TWIST

D TO D – WITH FULL TWIST

they are both too small to go around the Fat-Lady, and the Siamese Twins are joined together.' 'Don't worry,' I said, and tore one of the belts in two again, like this: (Tear once again, using the strip with the half-twist), and we had a belt big enough for the Fat-Lady. I took the other belt and tore it like this: (Tear the remaining strip) and we had two belts that would fit the Siamese Twins. For you see, we had two belts linked together, one within the other."

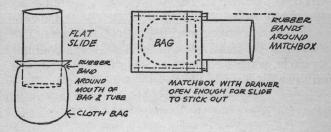

FLAT SLIDE

RUBBER BAND AROUND MOUTH OF BAG & TUBE

CLOTH BAG

BAG

MATCHBOX WITH DRAWER OPEN ENOUGH FOR SLIDE TO STICK OUT

RUBBER BANDS AROUND MATCHBOX

The Magic Coin Box

You vanish a coin, after it has been marked, and it will be found inside a small bag, which is in an empty matchbox, which in turn, is inside another small box. Both boxes are circled with rubber bands, and the mouth of the bag is also sealed with a band.

You will need several items to do this trick. First, you need a matchbox. Then go to the drugstore and get a powder or capsule box large enough to hold the matchbox. Make a small cloth bag about 2 inches long, and 1¼ inches wide. Leave the top of the bag open.

Make a slide (a flat tube) out of metal or very stiff cardboard, 3 inches long, 1 inch wide, and about ⅛ inch thick. This slide must be big enough for a quarter to slide through easily.

Now place the slide in the mouth of the bag, and

put a small rubber band around the top of the bag
and the slide. Wind it securely around the bag so that
it is tight. Place the bag and slide into the matchbox
but let the slide stick out. Close the box as far as possible. Place a rubber band around the box, both ways.
Put the matchbox in the powder box, and close this
up with a rubber band or two, going around the box
both ways. Of course the slide will stick out, but when
you pull it out, the bag will close, and the boxes will
also close tightly. Place this prepared package in one
of your pockets.

Borrow a quarter and have it marked by the owner.
Vanish it by any of the methods described in Chapter
3, "Tricks with Coins." Use any method you prefer,
but be sure you end up with the coin in your hand so
you can reach into your pocket easily, and secretly,
and drop the coin in the slide. After the coin has been
placed in the slide, pull it out of the box. Bring the
box out of your pocket, leaving the slide in your
pocket. Hand the box to the spectator who loaned you
the coin. Ask him to open it and identify his coin.

One good way of vanishing the coin is by the trick,
"The Dissolving Coin", page 27; or, the "Coin in the
Paper," page 29.

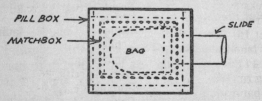

RUBBER BANDS AROUND BAG, MATCHBOX, AND PILL BOX

Index